Pathways of Autocratiza

Pathways of Autocratization addresses contemporary global politics' one of the most important questions: how does a country regress from a democracy to an autocracy?

This book offers a novel framework for understanding the processes that erode democracy and lead to autocracy and explains a specific instance of democratic backsliding in Bangladesh, the world's eighth-most populous country. With a probing analysis of events and trends in Bangladeshi politics, especially since 2009, the book contextualizes the country's autocratization process within global trends and compares it with others that have trod a similar path in recent decades, including Bolivia, Cambodia, Hungary, Poland, the Philippines, and Turkey. The book discusses the implications of institutional changes, the role of pliant media, the contribution of ideology, and the conduct of international actors in the autocratization process while also mapping future trajectories for the country.

Succinct, incisive, and thought-provoking, this book is rich in its theoretical robustness and empirical details. This is a must-read for anyone interested in understanding the dynamics of democratic backsliding and the prospects for reversing this trend.

Ali Riaz is a Distinguished Professor of Political Science at Illinois State University, USA, a Nonresident Senior Fellow of the Atlantic Council, and the President of the American Institute of Bangladesh Studies. He served as a Visiting Scholar at the Varieties of Democracy (V-Dem) Institute, University of Gothenburg, Sweden (2023) and as a Public Policy Scholar at the Woodrow Wilson International Center for Scholars at Washington D.C. (2013). His research interests include democratization, violent extremism, and Bangladeshi politics. His recent publications include *More Than Meets the Eye* (2022), *Religion and Politics in South Asia* (2021), and *Voting in a Hybrid Regime: Explaining the 2018 Bangladeshi Election* (2019).

Routledge Advances in South Asian Studies
Edited by Rani Mullen, College of William and Mary, USA
Founding editor: Subrata K. Mitra, Heidelberg University, Germany

South Asia, with its burgeoning, ethnically diverse population, soaring economies, and nuclear weapons, is an increasingly important region in the global context. The series, which builds on this complex, dynamic and volatile area, features innovative and original research on the region as a whole or on the countries. Its scope extends to scholarly works drawing on history, politics, development studies, sociology and economics of individual countries from the region as well those that take an interdisciplinary and comparative approach to the area as a whole or to a comparison of two or more countries from this region. In terms of theory and method, rather than basing itself on any one orthodoxy, the series draws broadly on the insights germane to area studies, as well as the tool kit of the social sciences in general, emphasizing comparison, the analysis of the structure and processes, and the application of qualitative and quantitative methods.

Works in the series are published simultaneously in UK/ US and India editions, as well as in e-book format. The series welcomes submissions from established authors in the field as well as from young authors who have recently completed their doctoral dissertations who wish to publish their first monograph under the care of the experienced Editorial Team.

For more information about this series, please visit: https://www.routledge .com/Routledge-Advances-in-South-Asian-Studies/book-series/RASAS

43. Urban Development and Environmental History in Modern South Asia
Ian Talbot and Amit Ranjan

44. The Changing Dynamics of Civil Military Relations in Pakistan
Soldiers of Development
Rabia Chaudhry

45. Deconstructing India-Pakistan Relations
Postcolonial Ontology and the Problematique of State Security in South Asia
Sanjeev Kumar H.M.

46. Pathways of Autocratization
The Tumultuous Journey of Bangladeshi Politics
Ali Riaz

For a full list of titles, please see: https://www.routledge.com/asianstudies/series/ RASAS

Pathways of Autocratization
The Tumultuous Journey of Bangladeshi Politics

Ali Riaz

Routledge
Taylor & Francis Group

LONDON AND NEW YORK

First published 2024
by Routledge
4 Park Square, Milton Park, Abingdon, Oxon OX14 4RN

and by Routledge
605 Third Avenue, New York, NY 10158

*Routledge is an imprint of the Taylor & Francis Group, an
informa business*

© 2024 Ali Riaz

The right of Ali Riaz to be identified as author of this work
has been asserted in accordance with sections 77 and 78 of
the Copyright, Designs and Patents Act 1988.

British Library Cataloguing-in-Publication Data
A catalogue record for this book is available from the British
Library

ISBN: 978-1-032-71199-7 (hbk)
ISBN: 978-1-032-71201-7 (pbk)
ISBN: 978-1-032-71204-8 (ebk)

DOI: 10.4324/9781032712048

Typeset in Times New Roman
by Deanta Global Publishing Services, Chennai, India

Contents

Figures and tables

Figures

Tables

Acknowledgments

I owe a great deal of debt to several institutions and individuals for their help and support while writing this book. A substantial portion of the book was written during my engagement with the Varieties of Democracy (V-Dem) Institute at Gothenburg University in Sweden as a Visiting Researcher in Spring 2023. I sincerely thank Staffan I Lindberg, Director of the Institute, for the opportunity. Thanks to Susanna Burmeister, Administration and Finance Assistant of the Institute, for her help during my stay in Gothenburg. The comments of the colleagues of the V-Dem Institute at my presentation and collegiality in informal meetings were encouraging. I thank Illinois State University for granting the sabbatical leave which enabled me to work at the V-Dem Institute. The ideas and arguments of the book took shape in my engagements with scholars on Bangladesh and activists inside the country. Although they are not named individually, their contributions were immense and deserve my heartfelt thanks. I am very thankful to Jon Danilowicz, a former US foreign service officer and friend, for reading the manuscript and providing suggestions. The comments of two anonymous readers of the manuscript helped to bring clarity both to the organization and content of the book. I owe them deep gratitude. Dorothea Schaefter of Routledge has always been supportive of my work, and this book is no exception. She expressed her interest as soon as she heard of my project and continued through the end. I cannot thank her enough. I am delighted that the book is included in the Routledge Advances in South Asian Studies series, and I am thankful to series editor Rani Mullen for enthusiastically suggesting the inclusion. Saraswathy Narayan, editorial assistant at Routledge, took care of various logistical aspects and attended to my demands. Lots of thanks to her.

Introduction

How does a country regress from a democracy to an autocracy? The question has become significant as we witness an increasing number of countries being transformed from representative inclusive political systems to restrictive exclusionary systems where power is concentrated in the hands of one person or a small group, state institutions are weakened, accountability mechanisms are decimated, and the rule of law is skirted. This book intends to offer an answer to this question by identifying the contributory factors and delving into a case study of Bangladesh, a country with a tumultuous history that embarked on a flawed and fragile 15-year democratic journey after experiencing a similar period of military rule.

This book has two objectives: offering a framework to understand the processes that erode democracy and lead to autocracy, and explaining a specific instance of democratic backsliding in the world's eighth-most populous country. As such, this book is about autocratization, "a process of regime change towards autocracy that makes the exercise of political power more arbitrary and repressive and that restricts the space for public contestation and political participation in the process of government selection" (Cassini and Tomini 2018, 15), and Bangladesh's political journey since 1991, the year in which it embarked on a democratization process only to later witness a serious debilitation of its fundamental elements, including freedom of expression, right to assembly, and open electoral process.

This brief introduction is followed by four chapters and a conclusion. The first chapter is divided into two sections, the first of which provides a broad overview of the global state of democracy, highlighting its downward spiral over the past 16 years. Saving a few bright spots, this has been an ongoing global phenomenon. The second section discusses the existing literature on the causes, processes, and consequences of democratic backsliding. As for the processes, three distinct approaches are identified: the structural approach, the strategic approach, and the institutional approach. Critically examining these three approaches, this section demonstrates that a common key weakness is their predisposition to institutions. In short, these approaches focus on how institutional decay contributes to the transformation, enabling would-be autocrats to use these institutions to achieve and stay in power. Instead of adopting

DOI: 10.4324/9781032712048-1

one of these approaches to analyze the autocratization process, I argue that this process has four components. In addition to the institutional aspect, other important dimensions are media complicity, construction of a legitimizing ideology, and external support. The third chapter makes a case for further exploring Bangladesh through a brief history of that country's democratic pathway.

In the subsequent two chapters, using these four interrelated elements as the framework, I show how they have contributed to Bangladesh's transformation into an autocracy. The first of these addresses the institutional aspects—that is, the three steps of institutional changes and the creation of a pliant mediascape through legal and extralegal measures. The following chapter examines the role of ideology and external actors.

The concluding chapter notes that the autocratization process in Bangladesh is not exclusive to the country but has also been witnessed in other countries which have undergone such changes, while also examining what makes the Bangladesh case distinct. The chapter also charts the way forward for Bangladesh.

1 Understanding and explaining the autocratization process

The world we live in

Overwhelming evidence and data are available that demonstrate that the world is facing a serious decline in democratic quality and that autocratization has gained pace in the past decade. Autocratization, defined as the "substantial de facto decline of core institutional requirements for electoral democracy" (Luhrmann and Lindberg 2019, 1096), has become a global phenomenon. The Democracy Report 2023 of the Varieties of Democracy Institute informs that "advances in global levels of democracy made over the last 35 years have been wiped out;" meaning "the level of democracy enjoyed by the average global citizen in 2022 is down to 1986 levels." The report further noted that in 2022, a record number of countries [were] autocratizing (V-Dem 2023, 6–7). Terminological differences notwithstanding, similar arguments have been made by other research organizations that follow the trends and patterns of democratic backsliding. Freedom House's 2023 annual report informs, "global freedom declined for the 17th consecutive year" (Freedom House 2023). The International Institute of Democracy and Electoral Assistance (International IDEA) stated in its 2022 report that:

> between 2016 and 2021, the number of countries moving towards authoritarianism was more than double the number moving towards democracy. During that time, 27 countries experienced a downgrade in their regime classification, while only 13 improved. The world also lost two more democracies in 2021—Myanmar and Tunisia. Moreover, 52 democracies are now eroding, experiencing a statistically significant decline on at least one sub attribute—compared to only 12 a decade ago.
>
> (International IDEA 2022)

In a similar vein, the Economist Intelligence Unit (EIU) report notes the continued decline of democracy worldwide (EIU 2023).

According to Freedom House, only 20% of the global population lives under a system which is "free" (Freedom House 2023, 30). V-Dem Institute's account shows that 13% of the people in the global population live in a "liberal

DOI: 10.4324/9781032712048-2

democracy" (V-Dem 2023, 11). The EIU report, which divides the systems into four categories (full democracy, flawed democracy, hybrid regime, and authoritarian regime), insists that only 8% of the global population lives in full democracy (EIU 2023, 3).

These reports show not only that democratic qualities are being eroded in democracies but also that authoritarian regimes are becoming even more repressive. International IDEA stated in its 2021 report that "the world is becoming more authoritarian as autocratic regimes become even more brazen in their repression. Of the 69 autocracies surveyed in the report, over half have become more repressive in 2021" (International IDEA 2021).

The gravity of the situation can be understood from the observation that Bertelsmann Stiftung notes in its 2022 Transformation Index:

> for the first time, the Transformation Index lists more authoritarian states than democratic states. At no time in the last 20 years has the BTI assessed levels of socioeconomic development and economic performance as being so low. The quality of government performance has also continued to decline, particularly with respect to the consensus-related aspects of governance.
>
> (Hartman and Thiery 2022, 4)

Hartman and Thiery add, "Over the past decade, nearly one in five democracies has experienced a steady decline in its quality of democracy" (Hartman and Theiry 2022, 5).

The regression was neither exclusive to any region nor to countries that had only embarked on a democratization path in recent decades. While regression was initially assumed to be a problem of emerging democracies, described as the "Third Wave Democracies" following Samuel Huntington's study (Huntington 1991), it was soon recognized as a global phenomenon.

In 2016, Mounk and Foa persuasively argued that democracy was also facing a serious threat in the "consolidated democracies" (Foa and Mounk 2016; see also Foa and Mounk 2019). In the following years, empirical evidence to the argument mounted, and institutions such as the V-Dem, Freedom House, EIU, and BTI provided data that showed the erosion of democracy in consolidated democracies. The BTI report mentioned the eroding pattern when it noted the global slide:

> This group even encompasses countries that were still classified as stable democracies in consolidation in the BTI 2012, including Brazil, Bulgaria, Hungary, India and Serbia. Since the middle of the last decade, Poland has been in this group, as well.
>
> (Hartman and Theiry 2022, 5)

In 2021, Freedom House reported that the United States' democracy was on a downward spiral. In that year, the United States scored 83 on a scale

Table 1.1 Overall Global Democracy Score, 2006–2022

2022	2021	2020	2019	2018	2017	2016	2015	2014	2013	2012	2011	2010	2008	2006
5.29	5.28	5.37	5.44	5.48	5.48	5.52	5.55	5.55	5.53	5.52	5.49	5.46	5.55	5.52

Source: Economist Intelligence Unit, Democracy Index Report, Various years

of 100, while in 2012 the score had been 94. India, once considered the world's largest democracy due to the number of people participating in the process, was downgraded in 2020. In 2021, the annual reports of Freedom House, V-Dem, and EIU no longer considered India to be a liberal democracy. According to the V-Dem Institute's 2020 report, India is an "electoral autocracy" (V-Dem 2020). It noted, "India is on the verge of losing its status as a democracy due to the severely shrinking of space for the media, civil society, and the opposition under Prime Minister Modi's government" (V-Dem 2020, 6).

This is not solely a trend of the past few years; rather, the phenomenon gained pace beginning in 2006 (Freedom House 2023, 3). Over the past 17 years, more countries' aggregate scores have declined than improved. For example, in 2006, the overall scores of 56 countries improved, while those of 59 declined. The year 2020 was the worst since the trend began, as a total of 73 countries' scores declined when only 28 improved. According to the EIU, despite occasional improvements, the overall global democracy score has been on a downward trend (Table 1.1).

While there has been a general trend of democratic backsliding over the past 17 years, a glimmer of hope seems to be detectable in 2022. The EIU suggested in its 2023 report that in the past year the global score has stagnated, which is viewed as a positive development considering the previous year's decline. Similarly, Freedom House's 2023 report shows that 2022 saw the fewest number of countries record a decline (a total of 35), while 34 countries improved (Freedom House 2023, 3). V-Dem Institute's 2023 report identified 10 countries which improved over the past decade, characterizing eight as "bouncing back" (V-Dem 2023, 28) and "making rare U-turns restoring democracy after a period of autocratization" (V-Dem 2023, 27). These data give hope but do not suggest that a large-scale reversal is in the offing, making it imperative to understand the current state of democracy on the one hand and the process of autocratization on the other.

How the phenomenon has been explained

Academics began to note in the early 2000s that countries that embarked on democratization processes in the 1990s were either stalling or reversing their course (Carothers 2002; Diamond 2002). The "third wave democracies" (countries which began their journey between 1974 and 2012) showed early signs of erosion and regression. By 2019, of these 94 countries:

> 34 experienced breakdowns, often in short order. In 28 cases, democracy stagnated after transition, usually at a fairly low level, and in two more it eroded. Democracy advanced relative to the starting point in only 23 cases. Few countries have succeeded in creating robust liberal democracies.
>
> (Mainwaring and Bizzaro 2019, 100)

The euphoria of democracy becoming the global norm expressed by social scientists like Fukuyama (Fukuyama 1992) and the claim that liberalism had emerged victorious against all other ideologies both turned out to be misplaced. An array of studies that highlighted the pathway of democratic transition either failed to address the potential for reversal or paid very little attention to the signs of discontent with democracy. The discontent in consolidated democracies highlighted by Foa and Mounk (2016; 2019) received the least attention. There was complacency that democracy was deeply rooted in countries where the majority of the electorate supported the representative form of government. These consolidated democracies were assumed to be immune to the malice of de-democratization experienced by those that had adopted the democratic system after World War II. The strength of the institutions in consolidated democracies was considered strong enough to withstand any assault, often coming from fringe groups or a small minority.

Increasingly, attention has been drawn to the emerging phenomenon of de-democratization. Three strands of literature emerged which deal with the trend, described variously as autocratization, democratic backsliding, democratic retreat, democratic regression, and democratic rollback. These studies explore the causes, processes, and consequences of autocratization.

The question of the causes of democratic backsliding gained prominence at the beginning of the emergent phenomenon and has continued to maintain high visibility (Cooley 2015; Kendall-Taylor and Frantz 2016; Tomini and Wagemann 2017; Jakli et al. 2018; Gandhi 2018; Waldner and Lust 2018; Lührmann and Lindberg 2019; Luo and Przeworski 2021; Diamond 2022; Carothers and Press 2022). However, relatively few studies have explored the question of how democracy backslides, or the process of democratic backsliding (Bermeo 2016; Levitsky and Ziblatt 2018; Andersen 2019; Warburton and Aspinall 2019). The consequences of democratic backsliding and autocratization are well documented in the annual reports of various organizations, for example Freedom House, V-Dem, and International IDEA.

The causes of backsliding/autocratization

There is no agreement among scholars as to what causes the reversal, whether in emerging or consolidated democracies. Scholars agree that there is no single factor; instead, there are manifold explanatory causes. Available studies highlight a plurality of causes.

In recent years, studies pertaining to countries which have experienced backsliding have proliferated. These regime-centric interpretations highlight the particular dynamics of a country and argue that a combination of events and socioeconomic structures contribute to the downward spiral. For example, in their study on Indonesia, Warburton and Aspinall (2019) argue that "constellation of structural, agential, and popular forces has led to an incremental deterioration in democratic quality." They further argue that the weakness of the nature of Indonesia's transition in 1988, the incorporation of anti-democratic elites into the governing structures, and the antidemocratic behavior of the two presidents are to blame for the current trend. Others have argued that "Indonesia's democratic backsliding after the 1998 Reformation could be attributed to the increasing polarization in society and the creation of problematic laws and regulations" (Haykal 2020). In a similar vein, in recent years, many authors have variously addressed the case of hunger. While Pap (2018) highlighted the legal and constitutional aspects which paved the road to an "illiberal regime" in Hungary, Scheiring (2020) provided a political-economic explanation highlighting the economic structure, especially the politics of capital accumulation and class compromise, as the decisive factor. These studies provide a wealth of data on the cases and help us to understand the processes in particular cases, but considering the many mediating variables, it is difficult to generalize their findings.

Other studies which have used multicountry examples have attempted to build a framework to explain the causes of and conditions of the backsliding. They have focused on domestic elements, which can be divided into three sets of factors: economic, political-institutional, and social (Riaz and Rana forthcoming). Poor economic and infrastructural development and higher economic inequality were described as the key proximate causes of democratic backsliding and regime transitions (Jakli et al. 2018, 274; Waldner and Lust 2018, 101). Diminishing support for democracy and the rise of populist leaders such as Donald Trump have been explained as the result of the middle class's economic hardship. The essence of this argument is captured in the title of Joshua Kurlantzick's book, "Democracy in Retreat: The Revolt of the Middle Class and the Worldwide Decline of Representative Government" (Kuralntzick 2016). Those who have underscored the economic factors have in large measure contested the received wisdom that economic growth fuels democratization, as advanced by Przeworski and Limongi (1997). Houle argued that "inequality increases the probability of backsliding from democracy to dictatorship" (Houle 2019, 591).

More studies on democratic backsliding insist upon, or at least underscore, political institutions as the key to understanding the phenomenon. The central arguments of the studies, which highlight political institutional conditions as the key variable, include a higher degree of fragmentation in the party system, excessive concentration of executive power, and poor institutional checks and balances. This line of argument claims that these factors tend to trigger democratic backsliding by creating instability in the political system (Tomini and Wagemann 2017, 7). Summaries of existing literature provided by Walden and Lust (2018) and Tomini and Wageman (2017) show that political-institutional explanations argue that the lack of accountability mechanisms, not only vertical but also horizontal, is an important contributory factor. The weakness or absence of accountability is intrinsically connected to the institutional configuration.

While the institutional explanation dominates the existing literature on democratic backsliding, the role of political actors or elites has also been significantly highlighted. As discussed earlier, regime-centric studies give greater importance to individuals; for example, an array of studies have pointed to Donald Trump as the central figure in democratic regression in the United States. Similarly, it is evident that Vladimir Putin of Russia, Viktor Orbán of Hungary, and Recep Tayyip Erdoğan of Turkey have played significant roles in their respective countries. As these examples are far from exceptions, researchers have explored the role of actors. These political actors or elites act to mold political institutions to undermine democracy. Gandhi (2018), drawing on the studies by Albertus and Menaldo (2018), Haggard and Kaufman (2016), and Levitsky and Ziblatt (2018), noted that democracy is reversed by unscrupulous elites who use institutions of democracy to entrench their political and economic power (Gandhi 2018, 11). Naim (2022) describes these new leaders as 3P autocrats, wherein these autocrats use populism, polarization, and post-truth work in tandem to undermine democracy. Notwithstanding the differences in the context of their rise, "their playbooks look uncannily similar," and their innovations have "deeply altered the way power is conquered and retained in the 21st century" (Naim 2022). These new autocratic systems are more personalistic in nature. According to Frantz and Kendall-Taylor, during the authoritarian shifts between 2000 and 2010, a staggering 75% of these led to personalistic dictatorships (Frantz and Kendall-Taylor 2017). However, analysts have also suggested that it is not only the presence of a single dictator that takes down democracy but also the complicity of a group of elites or beneficiaries. Referring to a de facto one-party state under the guise of multiparty system and apparently "soft dictatorship," Applebaum describes how the system works:

> This form of soft dictatorship does not require mass violence to stay in power. Instead, it relies upon a cadre of elites to run the bureaucracy, the state media, the courts, and in some places, state companies. These modern day *clercs* understand their role, which is to defend the leaders, however dishonest their statements, however great their corruption, and however disastrous their impact on ordinary people, and institutions. In exchange, they know that they will be rewarded and advanced.
>
> (Applebaum 2020)

The autocrats, who survive through such a strategy, rise using legal and constitutional means such as elections. For them, the constitution and elections are nothing but a "legal façade" (Luhrmann and Lindberg 2019, 1105). The social factors contributing to democratic backsliding include ethnolinguistic fractionalization, intergroup conflicts, and social class divisions. In and of themselves, these factors do not cause backsliding but act as contributory factors when they create conditions for social and political instability, leading to democratic backsliding. These social conditions have the potential to become the seeds for polarization and populism, especially when political leaders utilize them for immediate political gains.

The concept of populism has been variously defined. There are four approaches in existing literature explaining the concept: the ideational approach, the sociocultural approach, the political-strategic approach (Hawkins and Kaltwasser et al. 2017), and the discursive approach. The ideational approach is the most widely used in understanding the growing number of political movements in Europe and Latin America. In the ideational approach, populism is regarded as a worldview and an approach to explaining the world around individuals. Mudde insisted that populism is "an ideology that considers society to be ultimately separated into two homogeneous and antagonistic groups: "the pure people" vs. "the corrupt elite," and which argues that politics should be an expression of the volonté générale (general will) of the people" (Mudde 2004, 534). There are three elements to the ideational approach to populism: "people centrism, anti-elitism, and an antagonistic relationship between the "virtuous people" and "corrupt elites" (Ruth-Lovell and Grahn 2022, 2). As such, the idea of populism deals with concepts and categories tied to democracy. However, the relationship between populism and democracy has remained contentious and has been described as 'ambiguous' (Ruth-Lovell and Grahn 2022).

The available literature is divided on their conclusions: while some argue that populism is a threat to democracy, others insist its value is more as a corrective potential. General observations show that populist politics have been associated with different characteristics of the actors and their respective goals for the transformation of institutions. In Europe, populist politics is associated with the rise of right-wing political parties, while in Latin America, populism is often associated with the left-wing. Drawing on this observation, the conventional conclusion is that in Europe, the role of populism is more of a threat to democracy, while in Latin America, populists are trying to take corrective measures for democracy. Ruth-Lovell and Grahn (2022) tested several hypotheses about the impact of populism on democracy. Their empirical study has examined the relationship between populism and five models of democracy: electoral, liberal, deliberative, participatory, and egalitarian. It has been concluded that populism has negative impacts on several models of democracy. The negative impact is significant in the instance of electoral and liberal models of democracy. They also found electoral and deliberative models of democracy are more vulnerable to norm violations by populist actors (Lovell and Grahn 2022, 10, 13). Populism's impact on democracy is also measured by the International IDEA (Brusis 2019). In a comparison between populist and non-populist governments in power, it was found that "periods with populist governments in office entail declines on most aspects of democracy measured in the GSoD [Global State of Democracy] Indices data set" (Brusis 2019, 8). It concluded that "declines are significant for Elected Government, and for Civil Liberties and three of its subcomponents (Freedom of Expression, Freedom of Association and Assembly, and Freedom of Movement" (Brusis 2019, 8).

The concept of polarization is far less contentious than populism. It is defined in the Cambridge dictionary as "the act of dividing something, especially something that contains different people or opinions, into two completely opposing groups." In politics, a polarization among contesting opinions is an age-old phenomenon and is not viewed as deeply disturbing. However, the extreme version of such differentiation is highly problematic. This is described as "pernicious polarization." Defined as "the division of society into mutually distrustful us vs. them camps in which political identity becomes a social identity" (Somer, McCoy and Luke 2021), pernicious polarization contributes to the degradation of democracy. According to analysts, polarization "fosters autocratization by incentivizing citizens and political actors alike to endorse non-democratic action" (Somer, McCoy and Luke 2021). The relationship between polarization and democratic backsliding is borne out by available data. McCoy and Press, drawing on data from 1950, showed:

> severe polarization correlates with serious democratic decline: of the fifty-two instances where democracies reached pernicious levels of polarization, twenty-six—fully half of the cases—experienced a downgrading of their democratic rating. Only sixteen episodes were able to reduce polarization to below-pernicious levels, and the decline in polarization was only sustained in nine of those cases.
>
> (McCoy and Press 2022)

Polarization and populism, independent of each other, can create serious schisms within a society; they become dangerous when the two act in tandem. Luo and Przeworski (2021) insist on this line of argument. Under polarization, citizens seek to remove the incumbent regardless of the attractiveness of the opposition leader, and the incumbent stays in power by undermining democracy (Luo and Przeworski 2021, 9). Under populism, citizens knowingly or unknowingly consent to the erosion of democracy because they find the incumbent highly appealing, leading the incumbent to take free steps to bolster and concentrate executive power by undermining democracy (Luo and Przeworski 2021, 6–7). In such circumstances, incumbents appoint loyalists to key positions of power (e.g., the judiciary and the security services) and enforce censorship by buying independent media while legislating media organizations. The insidiousness of this strategy poses one of the most significant factors in democratic backsliding because it makes it hard to discern when a break with democracy occurs (Kendall-Taylor and Frantz 2016).

Consequences of democratic backsliding

As for the consequences of democratic backsliding and autocratization, the annual reports of various international research organizations such as Freedom House, EIU, International IDEA, and V-Dem offer comprehensive pictures. The 2023 report of Freedom House noted that in the past 16 years [2006–2022], democratic backsliding has undermined and weakened various aspects of governance and individual freedom. These include: Electoral process (with an exception in Asia-Pacific); Political Pluralism and Participation; Functioning of Government; Freedom of Expression and Belief; Associational and Organizational Rights; Rule of Law; Personal Autonomy and Individual Rights (p.14). Among these aspects, the most prominent decline has taken place in the rule of law, functioning of government, and electoral system. Freedom of expression, which includes media freedom, has shrunk remarkably. The report informs that "Over the last 17 years, the number of countries and territories that receive a score of 0 out of 4 on the report's media freedom indicator has ballooned from 14 to 33" (Gorokhovskaia, Shahbaz, and Slipowitz 2023).

V-Dem's 2023 report identified five broad aspects of democratic components which have experienced a decline in the past decade (2012–2022): freedom of expression; freedom of association; clean elections; liberal components; and deliberative components (V-Dem 2023, 16, Figure 7). Of these, freedom of expression has been hit in several ways. Government efforts to censor the media top the list of components which faced serious decline. Other components of freedom of expression include freedom of academic and cultural expression; harassment of journalists; media bias; and the media's self-censorship. The report states,

> Aspects of freedom of expression and the media are the ones 'wanna-be dictators' attack the most and often first. At the very top of the list, we find government censorship of the media which is worsening in 47 countries. […] Figure 7 also shows that the harassment of journalists is getting worse in 36 countries, … and media bias is spurring autocratization in 33 countries.

Repression of civil society organizations, considered part of freedom of association, has become widespread: "Civil society is similarly under increasing pressure. In 40 countries, governments are increasing their control over civil society organizations' (CSOs) existence ('entry and exit', and in 37 countries repression of CSOs is ramping up" (V-Dem 2023, 16).

These reports have clearly demonstrated the consequences of the rise of the new autocrats. It is worth mentioning in this regard that although autocratic leaders rise through an electoral system, they not only diminish the electoral system but also all kinds of accountability mechanisms. Both the Freedom House report and the V-Dem report highlighted the growing cases of manipulation of electoral processes. V-Dem report writes, "Now 30 countries are declining on this critical indicator, free and fair elections. A few years back, we found very few instances of governments undermining election quality" (V-Dem 2023, 16).

Processes of democratic backsliding

Given that the autocratization process is incremental and slow and that a single cause cannot be identified, there is no consensus in the existing literature on this topic. Instead, the existing literature suggests that multiple causes trigger multiple streams and mechanisms. It is also worth noting that at times these mechanisms overlap (Gerschewski 2021, 45).

The existing literature on the processes of autocratization can be broadly divided into three approaches: structural, strategic, and institutional (Riaz and Rana, Forthcoming). Table 1.2 presents a summary of the central arguments of these approaches and the list of authors contributing to each specific approach. The following section offers a detailed discussion of each of these approaches.

The *structural approach* seeks to understand how structural and contextual causes pave the way for anti-pluralist actors to assume power and undermine democracy, leading to democratic backsliding. Structural explanations can be traced to the works of Haggard and Kaufmann (2019 and 2021) and Luhrmann (2021), who demonstrate how structurally induced causes determine different stages or causal processes of democratic backsliding. For Haggard and Kaufmann (2019, 418; 2021, 27–28), three interrelated causal processes are associated with the reversion from democratic rule. The first stage constitutes social and political polarization that contributes to government dysfunction and a lack of trust in institutions, which in turn opens doors for autocratic electoral appeals. The second stage centers on to what extent the would-be autocrats can concentrate executive power by gaining legislative support.

In the third stage, executive powers are used to gradually subvert democratic institutions and curtail civil and political rights, making the process not only difficult to detect but also hard to counter until it is too late. These stages resemble the three ideal-typical stages of autocratization, offered by Luhrmann (2021 1017–1018). Structural and contextual factors contribute to generating "citizens' discontent with democratic parties and mounts (Stage 1), which enables adept anti-pluralists to rise to power in elections (Stage 2) and then to erode to the extent that is possible given existing constraints." The relevance of the structural

Table 1.2 Three Approaches to Processes of Democratic Backsliding

Approaches	Central argument regarding backsliding	Authors
Structural approach	Structural and contextual causes such as economic crisis, inequality, and polarization, open door for autocratic incumbents to assume power, who then subvert democratic institutions and limit civil and political rights to slowly destroy democracy.	Andersen (2019); Haggard and Kaufmann (2019 and 2021a); Gerschewski (2021); Luhrmann (2021).
Strategic approach	*Backsliding takes place through different elite-led strategies or modes of autocratization that limit political competition, restrict civil and political rights, and modify institutions surrounding the executive's preferences. The selection of the strategy is contingent upon context-specific circumstances and preferences of erosion agents.	Bermeo (2016); Cassani and Tomini (2019); Bajpai and Kureshi (2022).
Institutional approach	*Backsliding process begins at the hands of elected autocratic incumbents and occurs through the reliance on constitutional and legal changes and institutional reforms to consolidate executive power, to restrict political competition and media freedom, and to manipulate elections.	Levitsky and Ziblatt (2018); Ginsburg and Huq (2018); Scheppele (2018).

Source: Based on Ali Riaz and Sohel Rana. (Forthcoming). *How Autocrats Rise: Sequences of Democratic Backsliding*. Singapore: Palgrave Macmillan

approach and the above causal mechanisms can be found in Hungary, Turkey, and Venezuela (Haggard and Kaufmann 2019), as well as some extreme instances such as Nicaragua, Serbia, Ukraine, and Zambia (Haggard and Kaufmann 2021).

The *strategic or agent-based approach* highlights a series of elite-driven strategic moves that lead to democratic backsliding. Bermeo argues that the current trends in de-democratization follow three paths: promissory coups, executive aggrandizement, and strategic manipulation of elections (Bermeo 2016, 8). The agent-based approach received considerable attention in the analyses on both democratization and democratic breakdown, well before democratic backsliding and autocratization became a global phenomenon in the 2000s. In the 1960s and 1970s, the question of why democracies break down came to the fore, especially in the context of a growing number of coups around the world. In this context, Linz (1978) argued that personal attributes were a key factor in democratic breakdown. The general argument was that "under relatively unrestrained conditions," decisions by political actors shaped the trajectory—in both democratization and democratic breakdown. O'Donnell and Schmitter's (1986) highlighted the role of actors (especially leaders) in making the choices which paved the way for breakdown. They, however, mentioned that the choices were made due to the interactions of groups and interests within the government on the one hand and between the government and the opposition on the other. As such, while choices, particularly short-term choices, were influenced by various actors, the decisions were made by the leader—the agent. Capoccia's (2005) study on interwar Europe further explored the issue in similar kinds of political settings in several countries and argued that the decisions of democratic leadership determined whether the democracy would be sustained or broken down. Following Linz, Capoccia argued that "right decisions" saved democracy while "wrong ones" led to break down. It is worth noting that Capoccia (2005) examined the threats posed by antidemocratic parties within the political system. His analysis was about "short-term strategies that democratic rulers can adopt against extremist actors who use the guarantees and rights of democracy to challenge democracy itself" (Capoccia 2005, 4). While this analysis incisively explores the role of agency, it does not investigate the role of leaders who themselves are antidemocratic while gaining power through democratic means with a long-term goal of undermining democracy, a defining feature of the ongoing democratic backsliding/autocratization. This role of actors has been examined by Berlucchi and Kellam (2023). Their essay asks: "Who's to blame for democratic backsliding: populists, presidents or dominant executives?" The question presupposes that actors play the key role as opposed to structures. In their opinion, "populism provides ideological motivation," "presidentialism creates institutional incentives," and "supermajorities eliminate legislative constraints" (Berlucchi and Kellam 2023, 819–823).

The *institutional approach* is best represented by Levitsky and Ziblatt (2018). In their widely read book *How Democracies Die*, they explain how elected authoritarians shatter political institutions that were originally designed to protect democracy, thereby resulting in the slow death of democracy. Levitsky and Ziblatt (2018, 78–87) insist that democratic backsliding takes place in three subsequent steps: targeting referees; attacking opponents; and changing "the rules of the game." Unlike in the strategic approach, sequencing is of great importance in the institutional approach. Though scholars might disagree on the primacy of one-step before another in the sequence, they generally assume that democratic backsliding takes place in a sequence of distinct steps or modalities. For instance, like Levitsky and Ziblatt's (2018) three piecemeal steps, Ginsburg (2018, 355–357) and Ginsburg and Huq (2018, 72–73) offer five different modalities or pathways. These include the use of constitutional amendments to consolidate power and alter basic governance arrangements; the elimination of institutional checks and balances; the centralization and politicization of executive power; the degradation of shared public sphere by manipulating information in the environment and controlling the media; and manipulation of elections by eliminating or suppressing effective political competition. However, large numbers of democratic backsliding and erosion cases are explained using the institutional approach in countries such as Venezuela (Corrales 2015); the United States (Levitsky and Ziblatt 2018); Hungary, Poland, Sri Lanka, Thailand, and Turkey (Ginsburg and Huq 2018, 91–119); and Bangladesh (Riaz 2021 and Riaz and Parvez 2021).

The missing links?

These three approaches and the country studies over the past decade have enriched our understanding of various aspects of autocratization, identified various pathways of the phenomenon, and helped us gauge the possible trajectories. But these three approaches fall short in providing a comprehensive analytical framework to investigate the process of democratic backsliding. Three limitations are discernible in the studies that fall into one or all of these approaches and in most of the case studies. The first common limitation of these approaches includes their institutional bias. Although they have underscored different causal mechanisms, these approaches have viewed erosion and backsliding through an institutional lens. For example, a report by the International IDEA states,

> Democratic backsliding is initiated and driven by executive incumbents, legislative majorities and governing political parties. The process is relatively straightforward. First, they win competitive elections. Second, they form governments and use their power to weaken institutional checks on governmental power. Third, they modify the constitutional balance in their favor, restrict electoral competition and reduce the civic space underpinning political participation.
>
> (International IDEA 2019, 33)

A similar line of argument is made by the National Opinion Research Center (NORC) while assessing the democratic backsliding in Latin America. NORA's account of the sequences that lead a country to an autocracy has three steps (Table 1.3).

These accounts insist that targeting, reforming, and manipulating institutions by executive incumbents lie at the core of the democratic backsliding process. Changes in the constitution, executive aggrandizement, strategic manipulation of elections, and controlling the judiciary have somewhat exclusively received attention. This is not to say that institutional changes are not important, but it suggests that institutional changes alone do not contribute to democratic backsliding. Such emphasis has underestimated or ignored two crucial aspects: how the wannabe autocrats create support for their agenda to win elections and continue to cultivate the support while they remain in power; and whether domestic political developments are sufficient to explain the shift to autocracy.

Table 1.3 Three-step Pattern of Backsliding

Step 1	Illiberal leaders mobilize public support, win elections, and captures the executive branch.
Step 2	Once in power, illiberal leaders activate two reinforcing processes:

- **They capture state institutions.** For example, they use a legislative supermajority to pack the constitutional court.
- **They suppress the opposition.** For example, they use a loyal constitutional court to uphold laws that undermine independent media or opposition.
- **The two processes reinforce each other.** Institutional capture means fewer opponents to fight back, and weak opposition makes it easier for the executive to capture new institutions.

Step 3	When the two processes are very advanced, we observe a transition to autocracy. But:

- Illiberal leaders do not always pursue an authoritarian outcome (at least in the early stages).
- No outcome is predetermined; some backsliding episodes have been contained or reversed.

Source: NORC 2022. 'Democratic Backsliding and Authoritarian Resurgence in Latin America', p.2

While there is a preponderance of studies that exclusively focus on the institutional aspects, some are shedding light on other aspects as well. For example, in an exploration of the sequences of democratic backsliding, Hellmeier et al. (2021) examined eight most outstanding autocratizers between 2010 and 2020 and showed that before formal institutions are subjected to changes, "media and academic freedoms, and civil society, are typically repressed first." They further noted,

Alongside that, ruling governments often polarize society through official disinformation campaigns disseminated via social media and by encouraging disrespect for counter-arguments from political opponents. Only then are formal institutions such as the quality of elections undermined in a further step towards autocracy.

(Hellmeier 2021, 1061)

It is my contention that the support which brings the leaders to power and subsequently helps them to be resilient is created through constructing and/or reconstructing an ideology. Ideology, in this instance, is understood as a set of ideas "by which men [sic] posit, explain, and justify ends and means of organized social action with the aim to preserve, amend, uproot, or rebuild a given reality" (Selinger 1976, 325). One of the key roles of ideology is to contribute to the process by which rulers strive to create legitimacy, that is, "the belief that a rule, institution, or leader has the right to govern" (Hund, n.d.). Rulers, both democratic and undemocratic, strive to achieve this through various means. In the case of authoritarian rulers, such an endeavor is often beyond the usual authoritarian mode of governance, which is using coercion to silence the citizens. Given that the newly emerged autocrats intend to avoid being portrayed as the "dictator," and that over the past years, autocratization process has resulted in a smaller number of closed autocracies but more instances of "autocrats wearing democracy garb," increasingly the legitimation process has become increasingly important. One of the defining features of the current pattern of autocratization is that the leaders who unleash the debilitation process come to power through elections. As such, they need to justify their assumption of power by convincing many electorates.

The second is the role of external actors in democratic backsliding in a country. While there has been extensive discussion on the global scene of autocratization, little attention has been paid to the impacts of external actors on the backsliding process. Huntington, in his seminal work on the third wave of democracy, noted that one of the five factors which contributed to the proliferation of democracy after 1974 was the "snowballing" (Huntington 1991), that is, the demonstration effect, wherein early instances of democratization was emulated by others. As a note of caution, he mentioned that previously two reverse waves were made possible, among others, due to "reverse snowballing," that is, reversal "triggered by the collapse or overthrow of democratic systems in other countries" (Huntington 1991, 18). The snowballing is indeed one aspect of the role of external actors. In this instance, no country is explicitly encouraging others to go down the path, but the emergence and survival of a new autocratic regime sends a message and creates an unwritten playbook that is then followed by the aspiring autocrats. There are indications that autocrats learn tactics from each other. The second way that external actors play a role is through creating a supportive nexus. In the past decade, autocratic regimes have come close to others in various ways. Anne Applebaum has described this supportive network as the "Autocracy Inc." (Appelbaum 2021, 2022). This is a metaphor she has used to explain "the relationships between countries like Russia, China, Iran, Venezuela, and Belarus." She went on to explain,

> these are not traditional ideological alliances. These are not countries that have anything in common. Nationalist Russia and Theocratic Iran and Maoist China and Bolivarian Venezuela, and, I don't know, Collective Farm Boss Belarus don't share common texts. They don't share common ideas of what is a good society. They don't have a common foreign policy. They have a very, very different sense of the world. But they do have one common interest, which is all of them have the same political domestic interest in crushing or restraining their own democratic opposition. That is

one of the ways in which they now cooperate internationally. They have a common interest in crushing democracy activism wherever it appears. They dislike the language of democracy. They dislike the language of human rights. They push back against it in the UN and they even seem willing to help one another crush their respective movements.

(Democracy Paradox 2022)

The third modus operandi of the influence of external actors in democratic backsliding is direct involvement in a country. Often, an autocratic country tends to influence a fragile democracy's trajectory and pushes towards a non-democratic path. Russia's interjection into Belarus during the 2020 uprising is a case in point. However, the nature of interjection can take different forms, such as remaining supportive of an autocratic regime for strategic, security, and/or economic considerations. India's relationship with Myanmar, especially its foreign policy turnaround from supporting democratic forces to engaging with military in the 1990s, is an example in this regard (Routray 2011; Buncombe 2012; Ayob 2016). Such a policy has continued after the coup of 2021 (Radio Free Asia 2022).

Cognizant of these lacunae in the existing literature, this book offers a different perspective to the autocratization process using the case of Bangladesh. In the following pages, I will argue that there are four elements in the autocratization processes in Bangladesh. These are institutional aspects, the media's complicity, the construction of legitimizing ideology, and external support. I will show how these elements contributed to the gradual decline of democracy, especially since 2009, when the country had a second chance to build an inclusive democratic system—the first being in 1991 after a popular uprising deposed the pseudo-civilian military regime of General H M Ershad after eight years of rule.

References

Albertus, Michael, and Victor Menaldo. 2018. *Authoritarianism and the Elite Origins of Democracy*. Cambridge: Cambridge University Press.

Andersen, David. 2019. "Comparative Democratization and Democratic Backsliding: The Case for a Historical-Institutional Approach." *Comparative Politics* 51 (4): 645–663.

Applebaum, Anne. 2020. *Twilight of Democracy: The Seductive Lure of Authoritarianism*. New York: Doubleday/Penguin Random House.

Applebaum, Anne. 2021. "The Bad Guys Are Winning." *The Atlantic*, November 15. https://www.theatlantic.com/magazine/archive/2021/12/the-autocrats-are-winning/620526/.

Appelbaum, Anne. 2022. "Autocracy Inc: How the World's Authoritarians Work Together." 19th Annual Lipset Lecture, National Endowment for Democracy. https://www.youtube.com/watch?v=ShMiOJdrtcM.

Ayob, Azman. 2016. "India-Myanmar Relations: From Idealpolitik to Realpolitik." *Malaysian Journal of International Relations* 4 (1): 62–85.

Bajpai, Rochana, and Kureshi Yasser. 2022. "Mechanisms of Democratic Authoritarianism: De-centring the Executive in South Asia and Beyond." *Democratization*. DOI:10.10 80/13510347.2022.2062324.

Berlucchi, Antonio Benasaglio, and Marisa Kellam. 2023. "Who's to Blame for Democratic Backsliding: Populists, Presidents or Dominant Executives?" *Democratization* 30 (5): 815–835.

Bermeo, Nancy. 2016. "On Democratic Backsliding." *Journal of Democracy* 27 (1): 5–19.

Brusis, Martin. 2019. "Conditions and Consequences of Populism and Democratic Backsliding: International IDEA Background Paper." Stockholm: International IDEA.

Buncombe, Andrew. 2012. "Did India Betray Democracy in Burma?" *The Independent*, November 15. https://www.independent.co.uk/voices/our-voices/the-foreign-desk/ did-india-betray-democracy-in-burma-8323487.html.

Capoccia, Giovanni. 2005. *Defending Democracy: Reactions to Extremism in Interwar Europe*. Baltimore, MD: Johns Hopkins University Press.

Carothers, Thomas. 2002. "The End of the Transition Paradigm." *Journal of Democracy* 13 (1): 5–21.

Carothers, Thomas, and Benjamin Press. 2022. *Understanding and Responding to Global Democratic Backsliding*. Washington, DC: Carnegie Endowment for International Peace.

Cassani, Andrea, and Luca Tomini. 2019. *Autocratization in Post-Cold War Political Regimes*. Palgrave-McMillan.

Cooley, Alexander. 2015. "Authoritarianism Goes Global: Countering Democratic Norms." *Journal of Democracy* 26 (3): 49–63.

Corrales, Javier. 2015. "The Authoritarian Resurgence: Autocratic Legalism in Venezuela." *Journal of Democracy* 26 (2): 37–51.

Democracy Paradox. 2022. "Anne Appelbaum on Autocracy Inc." *Democracy Paradox*. https://democracyparadox.com/2023/05/09/anne-appelbaum-on-autocracy-inc/.

Democracy Paradox. 2023. "Anne Appelbaum on Autocracy Inc." May 2023. https:// democracyparadox.com/2023/05/09/anne-appelbaum-on-autocracy-inc/.

Diamond, Larry. 2022. "All Democracy Is Global: Why American Can't Shrink from the Fight for Freedom." *Foreign Affairs*, Centennial Issue (October): 182–197.

Diamond, Larry. 2002. "Thinking about Hybrid Regimes." *Journal of Democracy* 13 (2): 21–35.

EIU. 2023. *Democracy Index 2022 Frontline Democracy and the Battle for Ukraine*. London: EIU.

Frantz, Erica, and Andrea Kendall-Taylor. 2017. "The Evolution of Autocracy: Why Authoritarianism Is Becoming More Formidable." *Survival* 59 (5): 57–68.

Freedom House. 2023. *Freedom in the World 2023: Marking 50 years in the Struggle for Democracy*. Washington, DC: Freedom House.

Fukuyama, Francis. 1992. *The End of History and the Last Man*. New York: Free Press.

Gandhi, Jennifer. 2018. "The Institutional Roots of Democratic Backsliding." *The Journal of Politics* 81 (1): 11–16.

Gerschewski, Johannes. 2021. "Erosion or Decay? Conceptualizing Causes and Mechanisms of Democratic Regression." *Democratization* 28 (1): 43–62.

Ginsburg, Tom. 2018. "Democratic Backsliding and the Rule of Law." *Ohio Northern University Law Review* 44: 351–369.

Ginsburg, Tom, and Aziz Z. Huq. 2018. *How to Save a Constitutional Democracy*. Chicago, IL and London: The University of Chicago Press.

Gorokhovskaia, Yana, Adrian Shahbaz, and Amy Slipowitz. 2023"Marking 50 Years in the Struggle for Democracy." In *Freedom in the World: 2023: Marking 50 Years in the Struggle for Democracy*. Washington, DC: Freedom House.

Haggard, Stephan, and Robert Kaufman. 2016. *Dictators and Democrats: Masses, Elites and Regime Change*. Princeton, NJ: Princeton University Press.

Haggard, Stephan, and Robert Kaufman. 2019. "Democratic Decline in the United States: What Can We Learn from Middle-Income Backsliding?" *Perspectives on Politics* 17 (2): 417–432.

Haggard, Stephan, and Robert Kaufman. 2021. "The Anatomy of Democratic Backsliding." *Journal of Democracy* 32 (4): 27–41.

Hartman, Hauke, and Peter Thiery. 2022. "Global Findings: Resilience Wearing Thin." BTI Transformation Index 2022. Gütersloh: Bertelsmann Stiftung.

Hawkins, Kirk A., and Cristóbal Rovira Kaltwasser. 2017. "The Ideational Approach to Populism." *Latin American Research Review* 52 (4): 513–528.

Haykal, Maula M. 2022. "Democratic Backsliding in Indonesia: Past and Future of Atrocity Crimes." *Konekstual.com*, July 14, 2022. https://kontekstual.com/democratic-backsliding-in-indonesia-past-and-future-of-atrocity-crimes/.

Hellmeiera, Sebastian, Rowan Colea, Sandra Grahna, Palina Kolvania, Jean Lachapellea, Anna Lührmanna, Seraphine F. Maerza, Shreeya Pillaia, and Staffan I. Lindber. 2021. "State of the World 2020: Autocratization Turns Viral." *Democratization* 28 (6): 1053–1074.

Houle, Christian. 2009. "Inequality and Democracy: Why Inequality Harms Consolidation But Does Not Affect Democratization." *World Politics* 61 (4): 589–622.

Huntington, Samuel P. 1991. *The Third Wave of Democratization in the Late Twentieth Century*. London: University of Oklahoma Press.

Hurd, Ian. n.d. "Legitimacy." Encyclopedia Princetoniensis. https://pesd.princeton.edu/node/516.

International IDEA. 2019. *The Global State of Democracy 2019: Addressing the Ills, Reviving the Promise*. Stromsburg: International IDEA.

International IDEA. 2021. *The Global State of Democracy 2021: Building Resilience in a Pandemic Era*. Stockholm: International IDEA. https://www.idea.int/news-media/news/democracy-faces-perfect-storm-world-becomes-more-authoritarian.

International IDEA. 2022. *Global state of Democracy Initiative*. Stockholm: Sweden. https://idea.int/democracytracker/country/bangladesh.

Jakli, Laura, M. Steven Fish, and Jason Wittenberg. 2018. "A Decade of Democratic Decline and Stagnation." In *Democratization*, ed. Christian W. Haerpfer. 268–283. Oxford: Oxford University Press.

Kendall-Taylor, Andrea, and Erica Frantz. 2016. "How Democracies Fall Apart: Why Populism Is a Pathway to Autocracy." *Foreign Affairs*. Accessed September 5. https://www.foreignaffairs.com/articles/2016-12-05/how-democracies-fall-apart.

Kurlantzick, Joshua. 2016. *Democracy in Retreat: The Revolt of the Middle Class and the Worldwide Decline of Representative Government*. New Haven, CT: Yale University Press.

Levitsky, Steven, and Daniel Ziblatt. 2018. *How Democracies Die*. New York: Crown.

Linz, Juan. 1978. *The Breakdown of Democratic Regimes: Crisis, Breakdown, and Reequilibration*. Baltimore, MD: Johns Hopkins University Press.

Luhrmann, Anna. 2021. "Disrupting the Autocratization Sequence: Towards Democratic Resilience." *Democratization* 28 (5): 1017–1039.

Luo, Zhaotian, and Adam Przeworski. 2021. "Democracy and Its Vulnerabilities: Dynamics of Democratic Backsliding." Available at SSRN: http://dx.doi.org/10.2139/ssrn.3469373.

Lurhmann, Anna, and Staffan Lindberg. 2019. "A Third Wave of Autocratization Is Here: What Is New About It?" *Democratization* 26 (7): 1095–1113.

Mainwaring, Scott, and Fernando Bizzaro. 2019. "The Fates of Third Wave Democracies." *Journal of Democracy* 30 (1): 99–113.

Mccoy, Jennifer, and Benjamin Press. 2022. "What Happens When Democracies Become Perniciously Polarized?" Carnegie Endowment for International Peace, January 18. https://carnegieendowment.org/2022/01/18/what-happens-when-democracies-become-perniciously-polarized-pub-86190.

Mounk, Yascha, and Roberto Stefan Foa. 2016. "The Danger of Deconsolidation: The Democratic Disconnect." *Journal of Democracy* 27 (3): 5–17.

Mounk, Yascha, and Roberto Stefan Foa. 2019. "Democratic Deconsolidation in Developed Democracies, 1995–2018." CES Open Forum Series 2018–2019, Minda de Gunzburg Center for European Studies (CES), Harvard University. Boston, MA; Harvard University. http://aei.pitt.edu/102389/1/Working-Paper-PDF-Democratic-Deconsolidation-in-Developed-Democracies-1995-2018.pdf.

Mudde, Cas. 2004. "The Populist Zeitgeist." *Government and Opposition* 39 (4): 542–563.

Naim, Moisés. 2022. *The Revenge of Power: How Autocrats Are Reinventing Politics for the 21st Century*. New York: St. Martin's Press.

NORC. 2022. *Democratic Backsliding and Authoritarian Resurgence in Latin America*. Chicago, IL: University of Chicago. https://www.norc.org/content/dam/norc-org/pdfs/Democratic%20Backsliding%20Panel%20-%20Brief%20-%20English.pdf.

O'Donnell, Guillermo, and Philippe C. Schmitter, eds. 1986. *Transitions from Authoritarian Rule: Tentative Conclusions about Uncertain Democracies*. Baltimore, MD: Johns Hopkins University Press.

Pap, Andras L. 2018. *Democratic Decline in Hungary: Law and Society in an Illiberal Democracy*. London: Routledge.

Przeworski, Adam, and Fernando Limongi. 1997. "Modernization: Theory and Facts." *World Politics* 49 (2): 155–183.

Radio Free Asia (RFA). 2022. "India Is Keeping Close Ties with Myanmar, Even Transferring Weapons, NGOs Say." February 22. https://www.rfa.org/english/news/myanmar/india-burma-02222023180530.html.

Riaz, Ali. 2021. "The Pathway of Democratic Backsliding in Bangladesh." *Democratization* 28 (1): 179–197.

Riaz, Ali, and Saimum Parvez. 2021. "Anatomy of a Rigged Election." *Democratization* 28 (4): 801–820.

Riaz, Ali, and Md Sohel Rana. Forthcoming. *How Autocrats Rise? Sequences of Democratic Backsliding*. Singapore: Palgrave Macmillan.

Routray, Bibhu Prasad. 2011. "India-Myanmar Relations: Triumph of Pragmatism." *Jindal Journal of International Affairs* 1 (1): 299–321.

Ruth-Lovell, Saskia Pauline, and Sandra Grahn. 2022. "Threat or Corrective to Democracy? The Relationship Between Populism and Different Models of

Democracy." *European Journal of Political Research*. https://doi.org/10.1111/1475 -6765.12564.

Scheiring, Gabor. 2020. *The Retreat of Liberal Democracy: Authoritarian Capitalism and the Accumulative State in Hungary*. New York: Palgrave Macmillan.

Scheppele, Kim L. 2018. "Autocratic Legalism." *The University of Chicago Law Review* 85 (2): 545–584.

Selinger, Martin. 1976. *Ideology and Politics*. Croes nest, Australia: Allen and Unwin.

Somer, Murat, Jennifer L. McCoy, and Russell E. Luke. 2021. "Pernicious Polarization, Autocratization and Opposition Strategies." *Democratization* 28 (5): 929–948.

Tomini, Luca, and Claudius Wagemann. 2017. "Varieties of Contemporary Democratic Breakdown and Regression: A Comparative Analysis." *European Journal of Political Research* 57 (3): 687–716.

V-Dem. 2020. *Autocratization Surges, Resistance Grows: Democracy Report 2020*. Gothenburg: Varieties of Democracy Institute.

V-Dem. 2023. *Democracy Report 2023: Defiance in the Face of Autocratization*. Gothenburg: Varieties of Democracy Institute, Department of Political Science. University of Gothenburg.

Waldner, David, and Ellen Lust. 2018. "Unwelcome Change: Coming to Terms with Democratic Backsliding." *Annual Review of Political Science* 21: 93–113.

Warburton, Eve, and Edward Aspinall. 2019. "Explaining Indonesia's Democratic Regression." *Contemporary Southeast Asia* 41 (2): 255–285.

2 Why Bangladesh warrants attention?

The growing literature on democratic backsliding and autocratization has paid little attention to Bangladesh, a country in South Asia that joined the "Third Wave" of democracy in 1991 with the downfall of the military regime, but has increasingly veered toward autocracy over the past decade. The ostensible economic success of the country, measured both by the Gross Domestic Product (GDP) and the decline in poverty, matched with progression in social indicators such as reducing child and maternal mortality and enhancing education for girls, received coverage in international media and policy discourse. Remarkable economic growth despite the absence of good governance, lack of natural resources, and heightened fractious politics engendered the phrase "Bangladesh paradox" in the 1990s (Hossain 2017; ESID 2017). The country not only drew attention by becoming the world's second-largest producer of ready-made garments (RMG), but also because its garments industry provided jobs to millions of women who had previously remained either in the informal sector or marginalized. Economic growth and social developments took off in the early 1990s after the country embarked on a democratic path, and both economic liberalization and globalization became the hallmarks of the economy. Since 2017, Bangladesh has been applauded for its humanitarian efforts in sheltering more than a million Rohingya refugees from neighboring Myanmar. Despite these significant successes, however, data regarding the country's system of governance documented by the institutions that track democracy around the world continued to reveal a worrying development. These showed that Bangladesh is moving away from the democratic path under the Sheikh Hasina regime (2009–to date).

POLITY IV data between 1991 and 2018 documented a precipitous decline in the overall score after 2012. Between 1991 and 2006, the country scored a healthy 6 points. After a democratic hiatus of two years, when the country was ruled by a military-backed interim government, there was a significant improvement until 2012. But since then, it went on a free fall and reached a negative 6 by 2018. Consequently, competitiveness in participation and political participation experienced a significant decline (Figure 2.1).

Bertelsmann Transformation Index (BTI, 2022a) data on political participation shows that between 2005 and 2021, the score has halved in a range

DOI: 10.4324/9781032712048-3

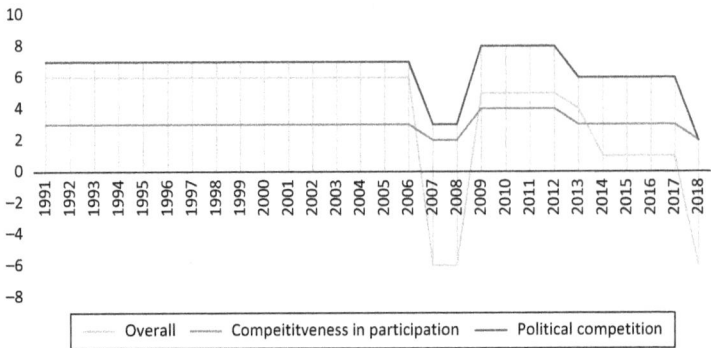

Figure 2.1 Democracy Score, Competitiveness in Participation, and Political Competition, 1991–2018.

Source: Polity IV, "Annual Polity IV Annual Time Series 1800–2018," Regime Authority Characteristics and Transitions Datasets, Center for the Peace. https://www.systemicpeace.org/inscrdata.html acc

between 1 and 10 (most democratic). The score combines information on the extent to which elections are free and fair, democratically elected leaders have the effective power to govern, and citizens have the freedoms of association and expression (Figure 2.2).

Boix et al. (2013) classify regimes on a binary of 0 and 1 scale, wherein 1 is considered a democracy and 0 denotes nondemocracies; Bangladesh has been labeled as a non-democracy since 2014 (Our World in Data 2023). Similarly, since then, International IDEA has described Bangladesh as an authoritarian regime. As the situation began to worsen, there were concerns about the country's trajectory. The Strategic Forecast predicted in 2016 that the country would shift toward single-party authoritarianism (Strategic Forecast 2016). Also, ahead of the 2018 election, international media warned of the accelerating pace of authoritarianism (Economist 2018). The change is most vividly captured in the institutional autocracy indicator of the V-Dem database (Figure 2.3).

It is against this remarkable pace of autocratization that various international organizations and analysts began to categorize the country as a "hybrid regime" (Riaz 2019), "authoritarian" (Savoia and Asadullah 2019; Blair 2020; Hossain 2020), "competitive authoritarian" (Mostofa and Subedia 2021), "moderate autocracy" (BTI 2022b), and "autocracy" (Riaz 2022). International IDEA continues to describe it as an "autocratic regime" (International IDEA 2022). This precipitous decline and indications of further slide toward autocracy did not receive much attention in international media until the United States' decision to not invite Bangladesh to the Democracy Summit held in December 2021 and the imposition of sanctions on the elite

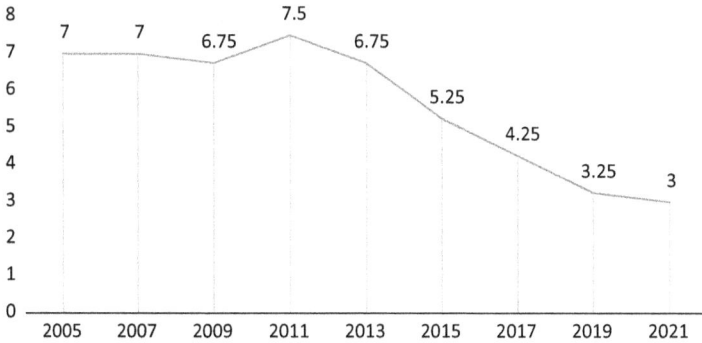

Figure 2.2 Political Participation, 2005–2021

Source: Our World in Data, 2022. "Political Participation." https://ourworldindata.org/grapher/political-participation-bti?tab=chart&country=~BGD

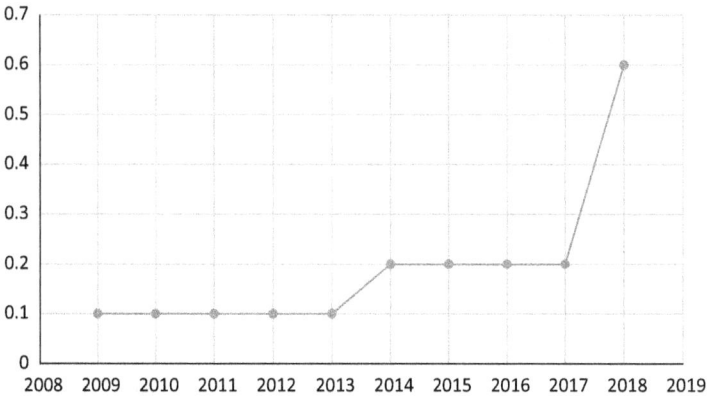

Figure 2.3 Institutionalized Autocracy

Source: V-Dem Institute Database, Version 12.

police force called the Rapid Action Battalion and a few of its officials (US Department of Treasury 2021). Economic crises that began to unfold in the summer of 2023 provided international media with the opportunity to explore further and highlight the regime's growing autocratic penchant (Economist 2023).

The data presented in the preceding description calls for attention and exploration of the pathway to autocracy in Bangladesh. The figures have shown that the country's turn to autocracy began in 2011, three years after the current regime came to power in a free and fair election. It is to a great extent a typical case of democratic backsliding when the elected leaders engage in the debilitation of state institutions; however, there are two aspects that need to be discussed to understand the significance of the Bangladesh case. First, as Bangladesh's democratic journey began at the height of the third wave of democracy in 1991, the Bangladesh experience of backsliding adds to the body of knowledge which has investigated the state of third wave democracies. It may provide clues to the fate of other countries where democracy has been stalled or reversed. The second aspect is the electoral dimension of democracy. Huntington's famous assertion that "two turnover test" (Huntington 1991, 267) is a key to the democratic transition has been invalidated. Huntington's (1991) central argument was that a successful turnover after national elections marks progression toward consolidation. If the party or group that takes power in the initial election at the time of transition loses a subsequent election and turns over power to those election winners and if those election winners, then peacefully turn over power to the winners of a later election, it indicates a consolidation. But in Bangladesh, four fair elections were held after the transition in 1991 (that is, 1991, 1996, 2001, and 2008), yet democracy not only failed to be consolidated but also remained highly fragile, and by 2011, it began to reverse. In this context, the failure of democratic consolidation in Bangladesh can be attributed to the lack of strengthening of other necessary elements of democracy. Moller and Skaaning's argument is that a combination of three elements ensures the establishment of a liberal democratic system. They are electoral rights; political liberty; and civil liberty and rule of law (Moller and Skaaning 2013, 41). Previously, Linz and Stepan (1996) made similar arguments that strengthening the five arenas is imperative for democratic transition. These are civil society; political society; rule of law; bureaucratic structure; and economic society (Linz and Stepan 1996). As such, the Bangladesh case is another illustration that repeated elections, even if held fairly, do not preclude democratic backsliding.

These developments, however, need to be contextualized within the broader history of the country, especially its democratic journey.

Bangladesh's democratic journey

Bangladesh emerged as an independent country in 1971, and the constitution written in 1972 introduced a unicameral parliamentary system based on the first-past-the-post (FPTP) system with 300 directly elected seats. Despite the promise of liberal democracy, the country witnessed a rigged election in 1973, moved away from a parliamentary system to a presidential system, and turned into a one-party populist authoritarian state in January 1975 through the 4th Amendment of the constitution. This period, particularly after the 1973 election, can be described as an era of populist authoritarianism. The one-party government was replaced through a violent military coup in August 1975 when then President Sheikh Mujibur Rahman, most of his family members, and associates were brutally killed. A series of coups and countercoups followed until November of that year, and during one of these coups, four of Mujib's confidants were killed inside the jail after being incarcerated since August.

Over the ensuing 15 years, the country experienced military rule and several failed coups, witnessed the assassination of another President (Ziaur Rahman) in 1981, and saw the rise of another military leader (H M Ershad) in early 1982. Although General Ziaur Rahman officially became the head of the state in April 1977, he emerged as the *de facto* leader soon after the November 7, 1975, coup engineered by the radical leftist party Jatiya Samajantantrik Dal (JSD). During his tenure, Zia civilized his rule through various measures, including creating a political party (Bangladesh Nationalist Party, est. 1978) and holding presidential and parliamentary elections (1976, 1978). These provided constitutional legitimacy to his regime but were far short of becoming an electoral democracy as the military essentially held power. General Ershad followed Zia's playbook to the letter, including founding a new political party (Jatiya Party, est. 1986), but unlike Zia, who succeeded in cultivating a significant support base, Ershad failed to gain any substantial traction. He relied entirely on coercive tactics to remain in power, while major opposition parties continued periodic street agitations and boycotted most of the national elections. The 1986 parliamentary election, which was participated in by the Awami League (AL) and the Jamaat-i-Islami (JI) and boycotted by the BNP and left political parties, allowed the regime to put on a civilian garb and legitimize the coup. Yet, it remained military authoritarianism for all intents and purposes.

An eight-year pro-democracy movement that united all opposition political parties was spearheaded by three alliances and culminated in a popular uprising in December 1990, which deposed the pseudo-civilian military government (Maniruzzaman 1992). The uprising not only brought down the government but also brought an end to the era of civilian and military authoritarianism. The uprising raised hopes for democratization. By some measures, Bangladesh joined the third wave of democracy.

The expectation that the country would then move toward liberal democracy was based on the lessons from the pro-democracy movement, particularly an agreement signed by all political parties at the height of the movement promising to adhere to the fundamental canons of liberal democracy, such as fair elections, freedom of assembly, and freedom of the press (Figure 3.4).

Between 1991 and 2009, Bangladesh experienced the introduction of electoral democracy after the downfall of the pseudo-civilian military regime of General H M Ershad. Three fair elections were held between 1991 and 2008, when power alternated between two major political parties: the Bangladesh Nationalist Party (BNP), led by Khaleda Zia, and the Bangladesh Awami League (BAL), led by Sheikh Hasina. However, during this period, neither of the parties were inclined to strengthen democratic institutions such as the

Election Commission and were not supportive of horizontal accountability mechanisms such as heeding the criticisms of the civil society organizations. Judicial independence was promised by both parties, but legal measures to ensure the separation between executive and judiciary were not taken. Instead, judicial appointments, particularly at the High Court, were made based on political considerations. As such, the quality of democracy eroded, and constitutional and extra-constitutional measures were used to concentrate power in the hands of the Prime Minister. While in power, both parties tried to manipulate the constitution to ensure unbridled control over the electoral process.

However, a caretaker government (CTG) system, which was introduced as a stop-gap emergency system in 1990 and incorporated in the constitution in 1996, acted as the guardrail against large-scale fraud in the election process. The caretaker system was included in the constitution because of three interrelated events: first, the rigging of a few byelections of parliamentary seats by the incumbent Bangladesh Nationalist Party (BNP); secondly, the resignations of 143 opposition members of the parliament in December 1994, followed by violent street agitations led by the Awami League and its allies; and third, a parliamentary election held in February 1996, boycotted by all opposition parties. The system required setting up an interim non-party government headed by the past Chief Justice of the country for three months to oversee the election. In 2006, an impasse on who should be heading the next CTG government led to street agitation and violence. The contention emerged because the opposition AL was opposed to the past Chief Justice K M Hasan as the head of the CTG. Mr. Hasan became eligible because of a constitutional amendment made by the BNP in 2004. The change in constitution extended the tenure of the sitting Chief Justice, which in turn would make the previously retired Chief Justice head the caretaker government. The previous CJ, Justice K M Hasan, was a member of the BNP in the late 1970s before becoming a justice in the 1990s.

This deadlock led to a "promissory coup" in January 2007. Promissory coups "frame the ouster of an elected government as a defense of democratic legality and make a public promise to hold elections and restore democracy as soon as possible" (Bermeo 2016, 6). However, these regimes often continue to hold on to power for a long period, and the coup makers renege on their promises to restore democracy. In the case of Bangladesh, thanks to external pressure, a global economic crisis, growing popular discontent, and the inability of the regime to deliver on its promises of reforming the political system, the coup makers exited power at the end of 2008 through an election. The election delivered a supermajority to the Bangladesh Awami League (BAL). This marked the second beginning of democratization in Bangladesh.

In 2009, the BAL, led by Sheikh Hasina, was faced with two options. One option was to examine weaknesses of the democratic practices between 1991 and 2006, which led to the military's intervention to resolve the political crisis and two years of democratic hiatus, strengthen democratic institutions, including various accountability mechanisms, and create an environment within which electoral democracy could flourish. The alternative was to establish firm control over the state institutions, weaken the accountability mechanism, establish an electoral system that guarantees that power never slips out of its hands, and debilitate the state institutions that are essential for democracy. Fourteen years later, it is now evident which pathway the ruling party chose: a path toward the gradual decline of democracy, concentration of power in the hands of Prime Minister Sheikh Hasina, a legislature without an opposition worthy of its name, decimation of civil society, a partisan civil administration and a compromised judiciary. This process, as I will discuss in the next chapter, was incremental and achieved through institutional changes with the support of pliant media, legitimizing through an ideology, and with the support of a foreign actor.

References

Bermeo, Nancy. 2016. "On Democratic Backsliding." *Journal of Democracy* 27 (1): 5–19.

Blair, Harry. 2020. "Bangladesh Paradox." *Journal of Democracy* 31 (4): 138–150.

Boix, Carols, Michael Miller, and Sebastian Rosato. 2013. "A Complete Data Set of Political Regimes, 1800–2007." *Comparative Political Studies* 46 (12): 1523–1554. https://doi.org/10.1177/0010414012463905.

BTI. 2022a. "Transformation Atlas, Bangladesh: Overall Score." https://atlas.bti-project.org/1*2022*CV:CTC:SELBGD*CAT*BGD*REG:TAB.

BTI. 2022b. *Transformation Index BTI 2022: Governance in International Comparison.* Gütersloh: Verlag Bertelsmann Stiftung.

Economist. 2018. "Bangladesh's Slide Towards Authoritarianism Is Accelerating." October 4. Accessed June 19, 2022. https://www.economist.com/asia/2018/10/04/bangladeshs-slide-towards-authoritarianism-is-accelerating.

Economist. 2023. "Bangladesh's Economic Miracle Is at Jeopardy." March 2. https://www.economist.com/asia/2023/03/01/bangladeshs-economic-miracle-is-in-jeopardy.

ESID. 2017. "The Bangladesh Paradox: Why Has the Politics Performed So Well for Bangladesh?" ESID Briefing Paper 27. Effective States and Inclusive Development (ESID) Research Center, University of Manchester.

Hossain, Akhand Akhtar. 2020. "Anatomy of Creeping Authoritarianism in Bangladesh: A Historical Analysis of Some Events that Shaped the Present State of Bangladesh's Culture and Politics." *Asian Journal of Political Science* 28 (1): 13–39.

Hossain, Naomi. 2017. *The Aid Lab: Understanding Bangladesh's Unexpected Success.* London: Oxford University Press.

Huntington, Samuel P. 1991. *The Third Wave of Democratization in the Late Twentieth Century.* London: University of Oklahoma Press.

International IDEA. 2022. *Global State of Democracy Initiative.* Stockholm. https://idea.int/democracytracker/country/bangladesh.

Linz, Juan J., and Alfred Stepan. 1996. *Problems of Democratic Transition and Consolidation: Southern Europe, South America, and Post-Communist Europe.* Baltimore, MD: Johns Hopkins University Press.

Maniruzzaman, Talukdar. 1992. "The Fall of the Military Dictator: 1991 Elections and Prospect of Civilian Rule in Bangladesh." *Pacific Affairs* 65 (2): 203–206.

Moller, Jorgen, and Svend-Erik Skanning. 2013. *Democracy and Democratization in Comparative Perspective: Conceptions, Conjunctures, Causes and Consequences.* London: Routledge.

Mostofa, Shafi Md, and D. B. Subedi. 2021. "Rise of Competitive Authoritarianism in Bangladesh." *Politics and Religion* 14 (3): 431–459.

Our World in Data. 2023. "Political Regimes." https://ourworldindata.org/grapher/ political-regime-bmr?tab=chart&time=1991..latest&country=~BGD.

Riaz, Ali. 2019. *Voting in Hybrid Regime: Explaining the 2018 Bangladeshi Election.* Singapore: Palgrave Macmillan.

Savoia, Antonio, and Niaz Md. Asadullah. 2019. "Bangladesh Is Booming, But Slide Towards Authoritarianism Could Burst the Bubble." *The Conversation,* February 28. https://theconversation.com/bangladesh-is-booming-but-slide-towards -authoritarianism-could-burst-the-bubble-112632.

Strategic Forecast. 2016. *Bangladesh's Descent Into Authoritarianism.* May 31. https:// worldview.stratfor.com/article/bangladeshs-descent-authoritarianism.

US Department of Treasury. 2021. "Treasury Sanctions Perpetrators of Serious Human Rights Abuse on International Human Rights Day." December 10. https://home .treasury.gov/news/press-releases/jy0526.

3 Bangladesh's quiet slide to autocracy

Roles of institutional changes and media

As the Awami League (AL) came into power in 2009 after two years of military-backed caretaker government rule, there were few indications that Bangladesh would soon quietly begin to slide into autocracy. The AL's parliamentary supermajority was a matter of concern because, in South Asia, the experience of such tended to be inimical to democracy. Over the preceding 50 years, Bangladesh, India, Pakistan, and Sri Lanka had witnessed serious erosion of democracy and executive aggrandizement in almost all instances in which incumbents had secured a supermajority (Riaz 2013). The Awami League had secured a supermajority in the 1973 election, which enabled it to amend the constitution, moving away from Westminster-style democracy and introducing a one-party system. Despite this painful experience, there were hopes that the experience of 15 years of democratic endeavor and two years of hiatus would lead toward the strengthening of democracy, and not away from it. Unfortunately, the autocratization process began in 2011. The process comprised four elements: institutional changes, media's collusion, ideological legitimation, and foreign actors' support. The combination of all four elements, at times concurrently, contributed to the process. This chapter discusses the roles of institutional changes and the media's complicity. Two other elements will be discussed in the following chapter.

Institutional aspects

In Bangladesh, institutional elements of autocratization—including changes in the constitutional arrangements, manipulation of electoral process, executive aggrandizement, and use of legal measures to silence political opponents and civil society—had three stages. The process started with a change to the constitution, which allowed for a non-inclusive election, followed by the persecution of opposition leaders and limiting freedom of expression while targeting institutions such as the judiciary and law enforcement agencies. The sequences of the process are described below (Table 3.1)

In the first stage of the process in Bangladesh, the incumbent AL targeted the constitution. In 2011, the AL Parliamentary supermajority passed the 15th Amendment of the constitution, removing its caretaker government

DOI: 10.4324/9781032712048-4

Table 3.1 Stages of Autocratization in Bangladesh

Stage	Goals	Methods	Actions
Stage 1 Change the rules of governing. Legislation, constitution, and electoral system	• Ensures dominance of the incumbent over the election • Ensures a subservient legislative body • Enhances the power of the executive body • Executive branch becomes free from accountability	• Introduce legislature to favor the ruling party	• Removal of the caretaker government through constitutional amendment in 2011
Stage 2 Targets opponents of the government Political opponents, critical media, business leaders, etc.	• To demoralize and weaken the opposition • To dissuade criticisms of the government	• Bribery/Blackmail • Charge opponents with invented or exaggerated criminal activities	• Frivolous cases against the leaders of the opposition, particularly the BNP. • Amendment of the ICT Act 2006 in 2013, adding draconian provisions limiting freedom of the press
Stage 3 Target the "referees" of the state The judiciary, law enforcement, tax, and regulation agencies	• Ensure loyalty of the institutions, so that the incumbent can protect the government (ruling party and leader) and attack opponents	• Bribery and blackmail • Replace civil servants with loyalists • Impeach judges • Court packing (appointing party people in court) • Create new institutions	• Removal of the Chief Justice after annulling the 16th Amendment of the constitution.

Source: Author, based on Levitsky and Ziblatt 2018, 78.

(CTG) provision in order to establish the dominance of the ruling party. By abolishing the CTG provision, the incumbent removed uncertainty regarding future election results. All elections held under the incumbent in Bangladesh between 1973 and 1990 and in February 1996 delivered victory to the ruling party. The 15th Amendment ensured that the same results could be repeated by stipulating that the incumbent would oversee subsequent elections. The new arrangement opened the door for unchecked electoral fraud.

The ruling party and its allies used a summary verdict of the Supreme Court delivered in May 2010 as a pretext to enact this change, despite objections from members of civil society and opposition political parties. On 10 May 2011, the Supreme Court issued a short order for a verdict on a case challenging the constitutionality of the existing CTG system. The summary verdict stated that "The Constitution (Thirteenth Amendment) Act, 1996 (Act 1 of 1996) is prospectively declared void and ultra vires of the Constitution." But it also made the observation that "The election to the Tenth and the Eleventh Parliament may be held under the provisions of the above-mentioned Thirteenth Amendment" (Sarkar 2011, 1). Neither the summary verdict nor the complete one, which was made public 14 months later, unequivocally suggested completely scrapping the CTG system, yet the ruling party used it as a pretext to do so. Interestingly, the process of abolishing the system suggests that the decision was made singularly by Prime Minister Sheikh Hasina.

The process of amending the constitution, especially to look into the CTG system, began on 21 July 2010. The proposed committee to do so was established on this date and was supposed to have 15 members drawn from both the ruling AL and the opposition BNP. As the BNP did not send any representative to the committee, all 12 of the committee's eventual members were from the Awami League. In total, 104 of the 114 individuals from various walks of life whom the committee invited to present their opinions on the matter did so. The invitees included a former President, the sitting Prime Minister, three former Chief Justices, three former and current Attorneys General, five senior lawyers, and other professionals. After holding 27 meetings, on 29 May 2011, the committee unanimously voted to retain the caretaker government and recommended limiting its tenure to three months prior to elections. After its meeting with Prime Minister Sheikh Hasina the following day, however, the committee changed its recommendation in favor of abolishing the caretaker government system. While the PM claimed on 30 May that the court verdict had made it imperative to scrap the system, this had been mentioned neither during meetings of the amendment committee, which took place between 10 and 29 May nor was it stated unequivocally in the verdict itself (Riaz 2019, 143).

The 15th Amendment of the constitution removed the CTG system and stipulated that the election would be held within the final 90 days of Parliament's tenure (or within 90 days of its dissolution if this occurred prior to the completion of its tenure). It was implied that the incumbent cabinet would continue to serve up to the time of the election and that the parliament would continue to function during this period. This was contrary to the common practice of parliamentary systems around the world to ensure a level playing field for an acceptable election.

This was a classic move to turn the country into a hegemonic electoral authoritarian regime, a regime that holds "uncompetitive multiparty elections that are not free or fair," (Diamond 2022) where "there is never any uncertainty in the outcome of national elections" (Roessler and Howard 2009) and which "systematically ... render elections instruments of authoritarian rule rather than 'instruments of democracy'" (Schedler 2006). An electoral authoritarian regime, to ensure its access to power, effectively strips elections of their efficacy. As such, the 15th Amendment of the Bangladeshi constitution was neither a response to the abuse of the caretaker system by the previous government nor a consequence of the Supreme Court's verdict, but rather a way to render the elections ineffective.

The opposition parties, including the BNP, threatened to boycott the 2014 general election if the CTG system was not restored (Economist 2011). The international community repeatedly called for ensuring an inclusive election, and UN-brokered talks between the incumbent and BNP failed to yield any result (UN News 2012). The incumbent went ahead with the election which was boycotted by all opposition parties. The result, therefore, was a foregone conclusion. Ultimately, more than half of the 300-member parliament was elected unopposed, as the opposition parties didn't file any candidates (Ahmed 2014).

Although immediately after the election, Sheikh Hasina hinted at a fresh poll ahead of schedule (Burke 2014), this did not take place. With a new system in place and the result of the 2014 elections, Bangladesh became a hegemonic authoritarian system.

With the constitutional change completed, the incumbent entered the second stage: the persecution of opposition leaders, particularly the BNP. By bringing frivolous charges against them and engaging them in court battles, the incumbent succeeded in weakening the opposition. In addition, the incumbent targeted the media and civil society organizations. The most telling example of the persecution of the opposition was the number of cases filed against BNP Chairperson and former PM Khaleda Zia. Between 2012 and 2019, a staggering 36 cases were filed against her (The Business Standard 2020). Although the first signs of such an approach became visible after the caretaker government filed a series of corruption cases against both, Sheikh Hasina and Khaleda Zia later faced different fates. By May 2010, all 15 cases against Sheikh Hasina (some filed during the BNP government between 2001 and 2006 and some filed by the CTG during 2007–2008 by the Anti-Corruption Commission) were dropped or quashed by courts (BBC 2010), while the cases against Khaleda Zia remained (The Daily Star 2018a). A special court sentenced Khaleda Zia to five years in prison in February 2018 in a graft case

(Rashid 2018). In October 2018, without precedent, the High Court increased her prison sentence to ten years (The Asian Age 2018). Khaleda Zia's son, Tarique Rahman, was also convicted on these graft charges (Aljazeera 2016). That same month, she was sentenced to seven years in another case. To some extent, persecution of the opposition began concurrent with the changes in the constitution. In 2009, the government decided to appoint a domestic tribunal called the International Crimes Tribunal (ICT) based on amendments to the 1973 Act. The tribunal was intended to try those who committed crimes against humanity and war crimes during the 1971 War of Independence. There was broad support at home and abroad for the idea of trying those who committed crimes against humanity and participated in one of the worst genocides of the modern era, thereby ending a culture of impunity. Various international bodies, for example, the United Nations (Dawn 2004: D'Costa 2021, 144) and Human Rights Watch (HRW 2011), offered to help, and the European Union passed three separate resolutions in support of bringing the perpetrators to justice. However, after the tribunal was established without any international involvement and the trial process began, observers raised concerns regarding its fairness and procedural flaws. Any criticisms were harshly silenced (Chopra 2015). As most of the accused were from the BNP's ally Jamaat-i-Islami, many viewed the process as more of a political move by the incumbent than an effort to ensure justice for victims and bring closure to the bitter past.

Finally, in the third stage, the incumbent imposed control over various institutions, especially the court. In this regard, the ruling party not only packed the court with its supporters but also forced out a Chief Justice and pressed him into exile. According to former Chief Justice S K Sinha, he came under immense pressure from the ruling party and various intelligence agencies after the Supreme Court in July 2017 upheld the High Court's verdict that the 16th Amendment of the constitution passed by the parliament contravened the separation of powers and was null and void.

Subordination of the judicial arena is almost a prerequisite for the maintenance of a hybrid regime. Levitsky and Way argue that this is often done by means of bribery and extortion and, if possible, by appointing and dismissing judges and officials (Levitsky and Way 2002, 52). According to Brown and Wise, institutions such as the Supreme Court or constitutional courts tend to function not only as arbiters of constitutionality and legal principles but also as advocates of the current regime (Brown and Wise 2004). The 16th Amendment of the Bangladesh Constitution passed by the Parliament in September 2014, which empowered it to impeach judges of the Supreme Court for incapability or misconduct, falls within this kind of effort. The insalubrious rhetoric of the ruling party leaders after the amendment was struck down by the High Court (May 2016) and the Supreme Court (July 2016) is indicative of the mindset to establish complete control over the higher courts. This is what led to the "resignation" of Chief Justice S K Sinha, who also left the country (Dhaka Tribune 2017). The CJ, in his memoir published a year later, claimed that he was forced to resign and go into exile (Bergman 2018). Similarly, retaining the President's power of appointment, administration, and removal of lower court judges rather than granting this to the Supreme Court through the Bangladesh Judicial Service (Discipline) Rules 2017 contravened the spirit of the separation of the executive and the judiciary (The Daily Star 2018b).

By then, the civil administration was under the control of ruling party loyalists. Authoritarian rulers, particularly populists, usually have three options regarding existing public administration: wait on the sidelines, ignore it, or use it (Bauer et al.2019). In the first option, the authoritarian leaders choose to reject and avoid the established bureaucracy and often take a hostile approach to it. In the second option, they rely on a smaller group of people who are close to the leader and isolate the larger bureaucracy from the decision-making process, and occasionally, even from the implementation processes. They denigrate the civil administration, which eventually leads to a dysfunctional system of governance. The third option is to use bureaucracy as a tool.

Sheikh Hasina adopted the third option: using the administration to maintain her power. In some sense, this can be described as "state capture." In addition to appointing party activists in entry-level administrative positions, the incumbent coopted the upper echelon of civil administration through various means, including promotions, punishment for those whose loyalty was suspect, and increased salaries and perks. For example, between 2010 and 2020, there was a threefold increase in the allocation for salaries and benefits in the national budget (Islam 2020). This process reached such a level that the leaders of the ruling party repeatedly complained that the bureaucracy had become the linchpin of the government, undermining their authority (Riaz 2021). This is magnified by the unprecedented level of politicization of the civil service, which works directly under the Prime Minister instead of in a hierarchically organized structure. As one editor has noted, "Today, more and more decision-making rests in the hands of powerful bureaucrats who have greater access to the centre (*sic*) of power in the person of the PM, who, over the last several years, has come to rely more on the bureaucrats than on her political colleagues" (Anam 2023). This is a telltale sign of centralization of power, "away from decentralized structures, overriding the power and authority of lower levels of governance – be it provincial administrations, regulatory agencies, etc. – to make the national state, and by extension its authoritarian leader, responsible for major policy decisions" (Arsel, Adaman and Saad-Filho 2021, 264).

As the 2018 election approached, political and administrative structures were in place to help the incumbent. An election was scheduled for December 2018 under the incumbent Awami League government headed by Sheikh Hasina. The BNP and the enfeebled opposition decided to participate in the election, making it the first participatory poll in ten years. Ahead of the election, the Bangladesh Nationalist Party (BNP) joined an alliance called the

Jatiya Oikya Front (JOF) under the leadership of Kamal Hossain, one of the framers of Bangladesh's original constitution. But months before the election, fictitious cases were filed against opposition activists and the general public to create a climate of fear. In many instances, the Election Commission, without any foundation, canceled the candidatures of opposition nominees during the scrutiny process. The appeals process against the decision tied up these candidates in court, making it impossible for them to campaign. Opposition rallies were attacked by the activists of the ruling party, while members of the law enforcement agencies stood by as silent spectators.

On election day, polling booths were found to be under the control of the Bangladesh Awami League and its allies' supporters. Many voters found that their votes had already been cast. A BBC report showed that ballot boxes were stuffed the night before. In the following days, it became evident that such incidents were not aberrations but rather a country-wide pattern. What became clear through the election process was that the Election Commission, civil administration, law enforcement agencies, and the ruling party acted in unison to deliver a victory to the ruling party (Riaz 2019, 69–79). Such concerted actions were well planned through state capture; one analyst concluded:

> News coverage, reports from human rights organisations [*sic*], confidential party documents leaked by journalists, and unusually candid public pronouncements by ruling party members, some of which went viral on social media ahead of the polls, revealed the government's elaborate plans for voter suppression, aggressive policing, systemic arrests and detentions of opposition activists – all with the singular objective of managing the election in the ruling party's favour [*sic*].
>
> (Rabee 2019)

The extent of the manipulation and rigging in the voting led the *New York Times* editorial board to describe the election as "farcical" (The New York Times 2019). The *Economist* described the entire electoral process as "transparently fraudulent" (Economist 2019). Although the result was a foregone conclusion, the scale of the incumbent's victory was astounding, to say the least: the AL and its allies secured 289 of 300 seats. As such, by 2019, state institutions, the electoral body and the judiciary were so under the incumbent's control that they became tools in the autocratization process.

Pliant mediascape

On 10 April 2023, in a speech before Parliament, Prime Minister Sheikh Hasina blasted the country's most popular and largest circulating newspaper, *Prothom Alo*, describing it as "the enemy of the [ruling] Awami League, democracy, and the people of the country." She went on, "I am saying with regret that they [*Prothom Alo*] never want to permit any stability in this country." (The Daily Star 2023a). This was akin to US President Donald Trump's infamous tweet on 20 February 2019, saying that the *New York Times* is the "true ENEMY OF THE PEOPLE" (Grynbaum and Sullivan 2019). Sheikh Hasina's statement came in the wake of *Prothom Alo* reporter Shamsuzzaman Shams' 29 March arrest, which was followed by another case against him and his editor Matiur Rahman. Shams was picked up from his home by plain-clothed police in the early morning, just hours after a ruling party activist filed a dubious case against him. The case against Matiur Rahman was recorded at a local police station in the middle of the same night. These cases and Shams' arrest followed a campaign against the newspaper begun on 26 March by pro-government activists, journalists, and the media for alleged "misreporting" (Ahmed 2023).[1] This blatant attack from the Prime Minister betrayed her repeated insistence that Bangladesh's media was free to criticize her government (Dhaka Tribune 2022) and Information Minister Hasan Mahmud's claim that "media in Bangladesh enjoys total freedom" (The Business Standard 2022). In 2019, the information minister claimed that media in Bangladesh enjoyed more freedom than the British media (BBC Bangla 2019). These official claims are contrary to the state of media freedom depicted in the international press freedom organizations' annual reports for the past decade, which documented a serious decline in press freedom (Figure 3.1). In 2023, Bangladesh was ranked 163 among 180 countries by the *Reporters Without Borders* (RSF 2023).

RSF data show that Bangladesh's score has dropped dramatically between 2011 and 2023. In 2011, the country scored 57 points, while in 2023, the score came down to 35.31. In a single year, in 2022, the score declined by more than 13 points from the previous year. As for its standing, it dropped 10 notches, from 152 to 162 between 2021 and 2022, and 17 notches in five years between 2018 and 2023. The deterioration of freedom of expression is also noted in

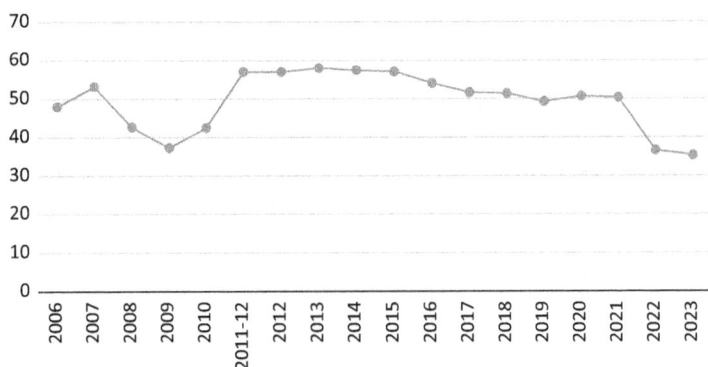

Figure 3.1 Press Freedom Index Scores, 2006–2023

Source: Reporters Without Borders, annual reports, various years

the Freedom House's reports of the past years; data show that there has been a steady decline since 2013 (Figure 3.2).

Developments in early 2023 also help to understand the state of media freedom in Bangladesh. On February 20, the government shut down the daily *Dinkal*, an opposition newspaper. The newspaper, with very limited circulation, served as the mouthpiece for the Bangladesh Nationalist Party (BNP) for more than 37 years (Aljazeera 2023). Earlier, in January, the Information Minister informed Parliament that the government had decided to cancel the domains of 191 online news portals. Alleging that these portals were engaged in "anti-state propaganda," Hasan Mahmud told Parliament that the decision was made "based on the information of intelligence agencies" (The Daily Star 2023b).

Understanding the state of media freedom in Bangladesh requires comprehending the modus operandi of information control under authoritarian regimes. In the old days of blatant authoritarianism, the relationship between the media and the government was hostile. The rulers tended to exert direct control over the media by keeping the media under the government's ownership and employing censorship. In these instances, censorship involved direct control over sources of information and clamping down on independent media where it was available. News and information considered "subversive" and those viewed by the dictators as "harmful" were largely precensored. Censorship was blunt, and the autocrats did not want to conceal their role in censorship. Often, this method of censorship was accompanied by "sanitized information" or "good news"— merely a euphemism for propaganda. The media were largely state-owned and controlled by the government; they were "His Master's Voice." Deviations from these were dealt with using punitive measures, for example, arbitrarily shutting down the media. However, technological innovations and the desire of the new autocrats to adorn themselves with the garb of democrats have made it difficult to tread that path any longer.

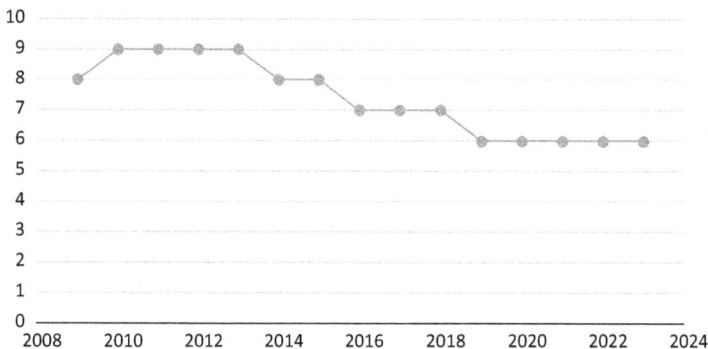

Figure 3.2 Freedom of Expression Scores, 2009–2023

Source: Freedom House, "Freedom in the World: Aggregate and Subcategory Scores." https://freedomhouse.org/reports/publication-archives

Therefore, the autocratization process in many countries has adopted newer strategies in lieu of direct and obvious control mechanisms. Essentially, these new strategies are meant to control the information flow in a more subtle manner. The subtler strategies and new measures not only tend to silence contrarian voices but perhaps more importantly, borrowing from Edward Herman and Noam Chomsky (1988/2002), can be described as "manufacturing consent." The new strategies are wrapped with legal façades, as new autocrats want to portray themselves as the protectors of law and justice. They often describe these as measures to protect the citizens from a small group of subversive activists and uphold national interests. Often, the regime conflates government and the state and labels criticisms of the government as "anti-state." In this regard, we should remember that the regime tends to label media, civil society organization, academics, and unions not only anti-national but also as working for "foreign powers – either consciously or unknowingly being manipulated by them" (Arsel, Adaman and Saad-Filho 2021, 263).

This is not to say that censorship and proscribing media have been totally abandoned, but it suggests that they are often avoided as bad optics. Instead, new laws have been enacted regarding media and information. These laws are harsher than anything before, with stricter punitive measures, and they are deliberately vaguely worded, allowing law enforcers to use them as they wish. These new laws can be broadly divided into three categories: anti-terror; anti-rumor mongering; and protection of the privacy of individuals in cyberspace.

The so-called Global War on Terror (GWOT) launched by the US and the West in the wake of 9/11 paved the way for these new anti-terror laws in the name of national security. However, the scope and nature of this legislation have taken various shapes in different countries, and they have been expanded over time. Those who joined the GWOT bandwagon used these new laws to silence their critics. The expansion of surveillance, electronic and otherwise, is an intrinsic part of the so-called "fight against terrorism" and at once imperils individual freedom of movement and expression. Over time, the media and freedom of expression have become the principal targets of these anti-terror laws.

The "anti-rumor mongering" elements of the new restrictive laws are either included in other new laws or legislated separately. China showed the way with an anti-gossip defamation law aimed at stopping "online rumors" in September 2013. In this regard, authoritarian governments use the courts as an instrument to justify their actions. In recent years, "spreading rumor" and "spreading fake news" have become synonymous. Since 2016, with the rise of Donald Trump, the concept of fake news found its way into mainstream discourse. Consequently, many countries have enacted laws related to "fake news."

These new restrictive laws not only impact the press but the entire citizenry. The threat of punitive measures or punishment looms large and creates an environment of self-censorship. Governments regularly target individuals and punish them for their unlawful acts. Punishment of individuals sends a clear message to media institutions, journalists, and private citizens where the line must be drawn. But the most consequential impact is to make self-censorship a common practice. Self-censorship, by definition, is not directly imposed by the government but undoubtedly results from the government's actions. This is not an unintended consequence but instead a deliberate regime strategy. It is a means of "strategic silencing" that ensures not only media subservience but also makes them complicit in the autocratization process. These strategies are employed in mainstream media but also extend to social media. The enormous control authoritarian regimes exercise over cyberspace has been described as "digital authoritarianism."

In addition to adopting the strategies of coercion and strategic silencing, the autocratization process includes an innovative way to limit criticisms of their policies while also creating cheerleaders. Levitsky and Way note that in many countries, the media are no longer under the direct control of the rulers. Instead, the rulers allow the proliferation of private media, "but major media outlets are linked to the governing party—via proxy ownership, patronage, and other illicit means" (Levitsky and Way 2010, 11). This has become the new pattern in various authoritarian and hybrid regimes. Loyal supporters and business enterprises are provided with media licenses while opposition and independent media face significant hardships. There are instances of government-backed ownership takeovers to silence critical outlets. These steps not only ensure a domesticated mediascape by limiting contrarian views, but they also shape political narratives. These narratives are intended to undermine the legitimate and critical narratives presented and investigations conducted by independent media (Riaz and Zaman 2022).

Bangladesh's media landscape presents a perplexing paradox as there is a complete divergence between the number of media and the dwindling media freedom. According to available official accounts, in the past decade, the number of both newspapers (dailies and weeklies) and television channels has increased significantly (Figure 3.3).

As of 2022, 2487 newspapers were being published, and 34 television channels were broadcasting. The government has issued No Objection Certificates (NOC, akin to a broadcasting license) to 45 channels, 11 of which have yet to go on air. Beginning in 2020, the government has required online portals to register with the Ministry of Information, and as of 6 June 2023, 367 online portals have done so. The government cites the growing number of media outlets as evidence of media freedom. But as demonstrated above, the plurality of media has not improved the state of press freedom; instead, the situation has progressively deteriorated.

In Bangladesh, two largely complementary measures created a pliant mediascape for the autocratization process to proceed: coercion and cooptation. The coercive measures include the draconian legal mechanisms and the use of extralegal actions to control media content. Cooptation measures include a proliferation of media owned by supporters of the government and unabashed support of the partisan media for the regime's actions.

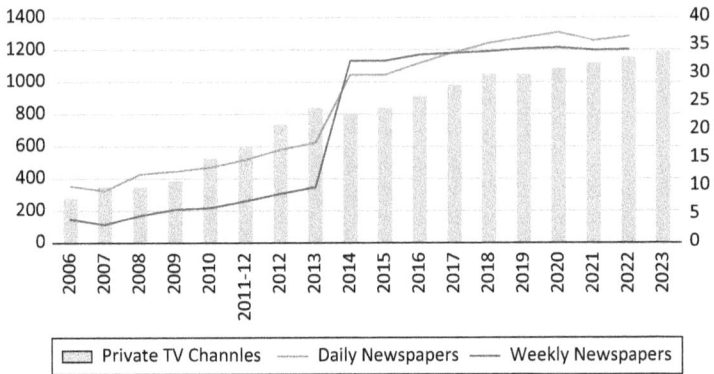

Figure 3.3 Number of Newspapers and Television Channels, 2006–2023

Source: Department of Film and Publications, Ministry of Information and Broadcasting, 18 May 2023.

The legal framework can be traced back to the 2013 amendment of the 2006 Information Communication Technology Act (referred to as the ICT Act 2006). The ICT Act 2006 had been intended to control the expression of opinions in cyberspace and was passed by the BNP-controlled Parliament in October 2006 (Bangladesh National Parliament 2006). The law provided the government with limited power to ban social networking sites. According to available analysis on the use of the ICT Act 2006, "only 426 complaints were filed under Section 57 from 8 October 2006 to 5 October 2013, and just a handful resulted in arrest or prosecution" (Bari and Dey 2019, 605). In 2010, a year after the AL government came into power, the government banned Facebook under two sections of the law: 46 and 57. Two lawyers subsequently challenged the Act's constitutionality in the High Court (SACW 2010).

In August 2013, as opposition to the government grew ahead of elections, the government amended the ICT Act through an ordinance. These amendments were later enacted by Parliament in October. These changes removed safeguards and procedural restrictions included in the original law, allowing law-enforcing agencies to arrest anyone without a warrant based on suspicion of committing an offense. For example, under the 2006 law, only authorized officers could file a case, and the case would be filed in the cyber tribunal. The 2013 amendments removed this provision, with the new Section 57 stating that,

If any person deliberately publishes or transmits or causes to be published or transmitted in the website or in electronic form any material which is fake and obscene or its effect is such as to tend to deprave and corrupt persons who are likely, having regard to all relevant circumstances, to read, see or hear the matter contained or embodied in it or causes to deteriorate

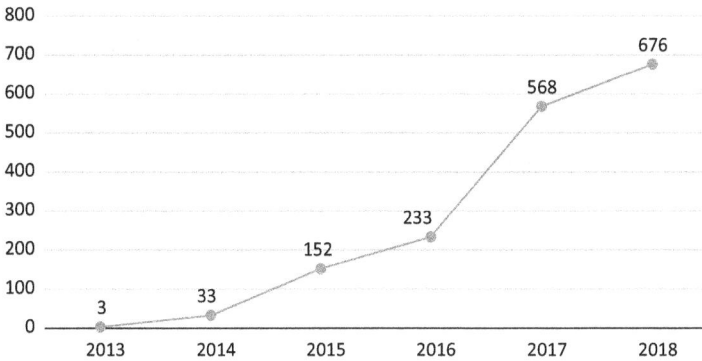

Figure 3.4 Number of Cases Filed under ICT Act 2006 (as Amended in 2013), 2013–2018

Sources: Asaduzzaman. 2020. "Digital Security Act: Over 1000 cases filed in two years," *Prothom Alo* English. 19 September. https://en.prothomalo.com/bangladesh/crime-and-law/digital-security-act-over-1000-cases-filed-in-two-years

or creates possibility to deteriorate law and order, prejudice the image of the State or person or causes to hurt or may hurt religious belief or instigate against any person or organization, then this activity of his will be regarded as an offence.

Subsequently, the law (particularly Section 57) began to be used wantonly. While the number of cases filed in 2013 was only three, it skyrocketed in the following years to 678 before some of its articles were repealed (Figure 3.4). A report by Human Rights Watch in 2018 noted that police filed 1271 charge sheets under the law between 2013 and 2018 (HRW 2018).

The amended law's impact on the press can be shown by the fact that between April and June 2017, at least 21 journalists were sued under it (Adhikary 2017). In the face of growing criticisms at home and abroad, in 2017, the government decided to repeal five sections of the law: 54, 55, 56, 57, and 66, while also introducing a new Digital Security Act (DSA) in 2018.

As the DSA was being drafted, it was reported that the controversial article 57 is "morphing into" the new law (bdnews24 2018). Various associations of journalists and editors of media outlets raised serious concerns about the draconian nature of the proposed law. International human rights organizations such as Human Rights Watch and Amnesty International and organizations that document the state of freedom of the press, such as the Committee to Protect Journalists, echoed these concerns. On September 18, 2018, the Editors' Council issued a statement explaining its concerns over the Digital Security Act, identifying some fundamental flaws in nine sections (8, 21, 25,

28, 29, 31, 32, 43, and 53) of the Act as a follow-up to their meeting with respective ministers on May 22, 2018. The government disregarded these protests, and the DSA came into existence in October 2018. The law's defining features include providing the government with absolute power to initiate investigations into anyone whose activities it considers a "threat." The Act provides law enforcement agencies with the power to arrest without a warrant, simply on suspicion that a crime has been committed using social media. It provides police with the power to search and seize without any warrant or oversight. Also, the Act allows the government to order the removal and blocking of any information or data on the internet it deems necessary, thereby providing broad scope to silence those critical of its policies or who share information on human rights violations in the country.

The law has used phrases such as "spirit of liberation war," which is not clearly defined, and thus provided government leverage to demean, vilify, and attack critics, alleging that they have undermined the spirit of Bangladesh's struggle for independence. Out of the 20 provisions of the law that deal with offenses and punishments, 14 are nonbailable. Five are bailable, and one allows for bail to be negotiated. The lowest sentence for offenses is one year in prison, and the highest is a life-term sentence, with most punishments ranging from four to seven years. These have been viewed by editors and journalists as creating a climate of fear. The nonbailable provisions of the law practically allow for indefinite pretrial detention for the accused. According to Law Minister Anisul Huq, as of 31 January 2023, 7001 cases have been filed under the law (The Daily Observer 2023). Analysis of 1109 cases filed between October 2018 and August 2022 showed that the law had become the weapon of choice of the government and its supporters to silence opposition, and a disproportionately high number of cases had been filed against journalists (Riaz 2023).

The press had already begun to fold under pressure in 2013. In April 2013, the opposition-aligned newspaper *Amar Desh*'s editor, Mahmudur Rahman, was arrested, and his newspaper was shut down. Rahman faced several charges and was refused bail for three years. After being released on bail, he was later attacked in court in 2018 while appearing for a case. In May 2013, police took control of the studios of Diganta TV and Islamic TV and shut them down for "airing misleading information" (Galhotra 2015). In January 2015, Abdus Salam, the owner of the privately owned Ekushey TV, was arrested after airing a speech by exiled BNP leader Tarique Rahman. In early 2016, Daily Star editor Mahfuz Anam faced 79 legal cases—62 for defamation and 17 for sedition—requiring him to appear at hearings in 50 of the country's 64 judicial districts (Sattar 2016). AL supporters filed these cases after the editor publicly admitted an error of judgment over publishing articles on "uncorroborated allegations of corruption against the current prime minister, Sheikh Hasina" (Sattar 2016) and Prime Minister Sheikh Hasina blasted Anam (The Daily Star 2016). *Prothom Alo* editor Matiur Rahman also faced similar legal harassment. Fifty-five cases were filed against Rahman for "hurting religious sentiment" after the newspaper published a series of articles on corruption in the purchase of power tillers by a local government office. These legal measures were accompanied by extralegal ones. For example, after *Prothom Alo* and *the Daily Star* published reports in 2015 on the Bangladesh army's killing of five men in the Chittagong Hill Tracts (a heavily militarized contested area in Bangladesh), the Directorate General of Forces Intelligence (DGFI) reportedly instructed their largest advertisers to stop advertising in both newspapers (Bergman 2015). This amounted to an estimated 35% and 25% (at least $1.2 million) respective advertising revenue losses for *Prothom Alo* and the *Daily Star* (Bergman 2015). Kamal Ahmed, who served as the consultant editor of *Prothom Alo* at the time of the government action, recalled the situation in the following manner:

> I recall the day I received a call from a senior official of an intelligence agency complaining about a story on a security operation in the Chittagong Hill Tracts. That same day, two top telecom operators, one multinational company and a few private commercial banks were forced to pull their advertisements from *Prothom Alo*. Many of those companies are still barred, albeit unofficially, from advertising in the paper. All those companies received verbal instructions they could not defy. It has become the new normal that such restrictive measures are imposed verbally, without any traceable records that could be used by the victims to seek legal redress.
>
> (Ahmed 2023)

Interviews conducted in January/February 2020 with 23 journalists, conducted for a study to understand the challenges they faced, revealed that intelligence agencies and the Prime Minister's Office press have been engaged in limiting critical media voices, particularly on television. Journalists have alleged that various state institutions (including intelligence agencies, the PMO's press wing, the police, and the Ministry of Information) have been instrumental in the government's effort to curb press freedom and silence critics. However, journalists insisted that members of intelligence agencies were known to create pressure if a media outlet or journalist published critical news. One respondent stated, "the pressure mostly comes from the intelligence agencies, whose officers extensively monitor newspapers and TV channels." Multiple respondents mention that if a critical report is published, either the journalist or their supervising editors will receive a "call" from personnel claiming to be members of security apparatus. If the news outlet or a journalist continues to publish critical news, they will face harsher repercussions. In addition, "officials in the Prime Minister's press team, the information ministry and influential pro-government journalists also exert pressure," a journalist told us. An editor said that after failing to intimidate them, members of such institutions followed his children to school and called his family members. The interviewee, in fear for his children, was forced to send them abroad. The omnipresence of the organizations has become such everyday knowledge that an editor, when asked which state institutions create pressure on journalists, looked around their office and said, "you already know who they are" (Riaz and Zaman 2022). A similar statement was made by a media development organization representative in a study conducted for USAID in 2022 (USAID 2022, 9).

The legal and extralegal measures forced the media to comply with the autocratization process. Cooptation and party loyalty of media owners and journalists also contributed to this process. As mentioned before, since 2010, Bangladesh has seen a significant proliferation of media, including print and online newspapers and television channels. Considering that television is the most popular source of information and most influential in shaping socio-political discourses, it is worth examining how a nexus between media owners and the regime developed over the years.

A 2021 study that examined 48 major media outlets revealed that many of these were owned by the leaders and supporters of the ruling party. For example, five television channels are directly owned by incumbent ruling party MPs. They are: Morshed Alam (RTV); Golam Dastagir Gazi (Gazi TV); Kamal Ahmed Majumdar (Mohona TV); Saber Hossain Chowdhury (Desh TV); and Shahriar Alam (Duronto TV). In addition, Salman F Rahman, appointed as the Private Industry and Investment Advisor to Prime Minister Sheikh Hasina, owns a major share of Independent TV and the daily newspaper *The Daily Independent*. In addition, No Objection Certificates ((NOCs, akin to license) for TV channels are provided to individuals and business houses which are close to the ruling party. Between 2009 and 2014, the government issued 29 NOCs, and between 2014 and 2018, the government issued an additional four. Examination of the owners' profiles shows that they are connected to the ruling party. With the connivance of state apparatuses, ruling party supporters have also acquired media that were previously owned by opposition supporters (Riaz and Rahman 2021).

The study found that 48 media outlets were owned by 32 business groups. While the nexus between large business groups under family ownership and the media is not surprising, what is deeply disturbing is that these individuals and groups are also engaged in business sectors that have received government patronage and support. Two sectors that have drawn enormous attention in recent years are banking and energy. The former has seen the spectacular rise of loan defaults by directors and large scams causing huge losses to the banks with the support of their owners, yet the government has not taken any actions against them. In many instances, defaulters belong to the ruling party. Since 2009, the government has regularly opted for an Independent Power Producer (IPP) model wherein the government has contracted with private companies for electricity generation, guaranteeing a significant amount of money as a "capacity charge" and at high unit prices. These charges have continued to be paid even when these power generation units have not provided electricity. The connections between business groups that have benefited from government policies and media ownership have undermined the independence and integrity of the media. These media outlets have often served as the instrument for rationalizing the slide toward autocracy by concealing facts and framing issues in a way that helps the regime.

In addition to media ownership, the partisan affiliation of journalists and media has been an important factor in creating the supporting environment for the autocratic transformation. Journalists' and media's affiliation with political parties began before Bangladesh's independence in 1971. Throughout the 1960s, as the nationalist movement grew in strength in opposition to Pakistani rule, many journalists tended to side with the Bengali nationalist forces, and newspapers showed their support for the nationalist causes. Likewise, some sided with the government and ruling parties. The tradition continued in the postindependence period with journalists becoming more aligned with parties, and political parties publishing their respective mouthpieces. Despite this trend, the journalist's union remained united, and respective party supporters tried to get elected to the leadership through fairly held elections to steer the union in their preferred way. The leadership of this union often alternated between supporters of various parties. However, there were allegations that union leaders were aligning with the ruling party and accruing personal benefits. Some journalists were coopted by the various regimes and offered lucrative positions in different professions, for example, state-owned media and diplomatic posts (particularly as press counselors in various missions abroad). Although the journalist union remained united in opposition to military rule, especially during the 1982–90 period, as in many other civil society organizations and unions of other professions, partisan affiliations became normalized. With the beginning of the democratic era in 1991, political parties, especially those in power (that is, the BNP and the AL), were as happy to enlist journalists as were the journalists to be so supported. Their affiliation not only shaped their activism beyond the profession but also influenced the tone and tenor of their professional activities, including the topics for reporting. This partisan attitude created a schism within the union and eventually brought an end to the united union. Eventually, supporters of two major parties—the AL and the BNP—created their own journalist unions at national and local levels. With this slippery slope, journalists and their union leaders gradually became the defenders of their respective regime's actions.

With a handful of exceptions, newspapers eventually became "supporters" of one party or the other. Both ideological affinity and perks (e.g., government advertisements and subsidized newsprint) lured first newspapers and later the electronic media into the ruling party's fold. These developments undermined independent journalism and the responsible, objective role of the media. Two years of democratic hiatus, between 2007 and 2008, did not turn the tide. To the contrary, the direct intervention of military intelligence agencies in controlling media content during this period seriously damaged the media's integrity. According to the journalists we interviewed in 2020, the heightened role of the intelligence agencies continued after 2009.

By the time the AL came to power in 2009, significant polarization had occurred within the journalist community, and the mediascape had become fragmented. The 24-hour news cycle, especially the increased number of television channels, accelerated the pace of polarization and accentuated the schisms. Interestingly, talk shows on various channels, a genre that began with the enormous potential of bringing various perspectives to the audience and offering informed debates, became a tool for pursuing particular agendas on almost all issues. In advancing the agendas, government leaning channels and talk show hosts use the platform not only to create a positive perception about the incumbent or shape an image of the individuals in power, but also to delegitimize the opposition and avoid any critical views. Some of the talk show hosts are alleged to be engaged in behavior tantamount to harassment of guests who hold a contrarian view.

The polarization and schism, as well as efforts to legitimize the incumbent and delegitimize the opposition, became evident during various crises, particularly during street agitations. The situation from March to May 2013 is a case in point. In March 2013, a movement demanding capital punishment of those being tried by the International Crimes Tribunal (ICT) for crimes against humanity in 1971 during the War of Independence emerged, primarily as a grassroots movement alleging that the incumbent has made an underhand deal with the Islamist Jamaat-i-Islami (JI). The movement was called the "Shahbagh movement," after the city square where the organizers conducted a sit-in for weeks. Soon the movement was coopted by the regime and used as a tool to propagate its interpretation of history, distract from the opposition's movement for a neutral caretaker government for the next election, and promote further polarization. A contesting social movement, led by an umbrella organization of conservative Islamists called Hefazat-i-Islam, emerged within days, describing the Shahbag group as anti-Islamic and demanding the introduction of an anti-blasphemy law (Zaman 2016). The coverage of these two movements created two contesting camps of media and provided legitimacy to the regime's heavy-handed measures in dealing with its opposition (Riaz 2017; Parvez2022). Similarly, media coverage of the road safety movement of the young school children between 29 July and 8 August 2018 demonstrated how the pro-incumbent media either disregarded or underplayed the atrocious behavior of the ruling party activists against the participants of the movement and journalists.

How political leaning, especially toward the incumbent, provides a different perspective and essentially exonerates unlawful acts is demonstrated in the statement issued after the arrests of the reporter of the *Porthom Alo* in March 2023. The Editors' Council, an umbrella organization of the editors of various media in Bangladesh, unequivocally condemned the arrests and filing of a case against Matiur Rahman under the DSA (New Age 2023), whereas the Editors' Guild, an organization which came into being in 2018, ostensibly because of differences within the Editors' Council, condemned the *Prothom Alo* for publication of the news which led to the arrest of the reporter and the case filed against Matiur Rahman (The Business Standard 2023a). The Editors' Council statement demanded the withdrawal of all cases filed against journalists under the DSA, whereas the Editors' Guild's statement held *Prothom Alo* in contempt. It says, "The controversial report published on the Independence Day on 26 March is akin to undermining independence." Additionally, condemning the publication of the news, the Guild statement said, "This is part of a series of attempts to implement an agenda in the name of journalism. Dissemination of fabricated and purposeful news is not journalism." The statement was apparently a retraction of its earlier position, which condemned the detention of the reporter by the police (The Business Standard 2023b).

The foregoing discussion on the role of media in the emergence and resilience of the autocratic regime demonstrated that persecution and the threat of persecution through legal mechanisms created a fearful environment leading to media compliance, but the compliance wasn't exclusively a coerced consent. Instead, ideological affinity and partisan affiliation of the media owners and journalists played important roles in the process, somewhat akin to the "willing executioners" of democracy.

Note

1 The so-called misreporting and an alleged "conspiracy" to undermine the country's independence concerned a report on the price hike of essentials published on the country's Independence Day, 26 March. A "card" used for social media promotion was posted on Sunday, quoting Zakir Hossain, a daily wage laborer, and highlighting a news report on *Prothom Alo's* Facebook page. Although Zakir Hossain's name and quote were used on the card, which said, "What is the use of this freedom if we can't afford rice?", a photo of a child who was also quoted in the report was attached. As the newspaper understood that a quote from the former and a symbolic picture of the latter could be misconstrued, it was removed from social media less than 17 minutes after it was posted. Later, the report was revised, and the amendment was mentioned and again published online. Nowhere in the report was it said that the highlighted statement was made by the child. Rather, it had been clearly stated that the quote belonged to Zakir Hossain. There was no factual error in this report. One can at best complain about not-so-apt visuals, but that, too, is a stretch, as using a symbolic picture with a report is not unusual in the media. Yet the newspaper considered it an error, admitted the "mistake," and corrected it in a short time.

References

Adhikary, Tuhin Subhra. 2017. "The Trap of Section 57." *The Daily Star*, 7 July. https://www.thedailystar.net/frontpage/bangladesh-ict-act-the-trap-section-of-57-1429336.

Ahmed, Farid. 2014. "Bangladesh Ruling Party Wins Elections Marred by Boycott, Violence." *CNN*, January 6. https://www.cnn.com/2014/01/06/world/asia/bangladesh-elections/index.html.

Ahmed, Kamal. 2023. "Making Prothom Alo 'the Enemy' in Bangladesh." *Himal Southasian*, May 12, 2023. https://www.himalmag.com/media-prothom-alo-the-enemy-sheikh-hasina-awami-league-bangladesh/.

Aljazeera. 2016. "Bangladesh: Tarique Rahman Jailed for Money Laundering." July 21. https://www.aljazeera.com/news/2016/07/bangladesh-tarique-rahman-jailed-money-laundering-160721073133821.html.

Aljazeera. 2023. "Bangladesh Shuts Down Main Opposition Party's Newspaper." February 20. https://www.aljazeera.com/news/2023/2/20/bangladesh-shuts-down-main-opposition-partys-newspaper.

Anam, Mahfuz. 2023. "Who Runs the Country?" *The Daily Star*, January 27. https://www.thedailystar.net/opinion/views/the-third-view/news/column-mahfuz-anam-who-runs-the-country-3231371.

Arsel, Murat, Fikret Adaman, and Alfredo Saad-Filho. 2021. "Authoritarian Developmentalism: The Latest Stage of Neoliberalism?" *Geoforum* 124: 261–266.

Bari, M. Ehteshamul, and Pritam Dey. 2019. "The Enactment of Digital Security Laws in Bangladesh: No Place for Dissent." *George Washington International Law Review* 51 (4): 595–631.

Bauer, W. Michael, Guy, B. Peters, Jon Pierre, Kutsal Yesilkagit, and Stefan Becker. 2019. *Democratic Backsliding and Public Administration: How Populists in Government Transform State Bureaucracies*. Cambridge: Cambridge University Press.

BBC. 2010. "Bangladesh Drops Leader Sheikh Hasina Corruption Case." May 30. https://www.bbc.com/news/10194392.

BBC Bangla. 2019. "তথ্যমন্ত্রী হাছান মাহমুদ বলেছেন - যুক্তরাজ্যের চেয়ে বাংলাদেশে গণমাধ্যমের স্বাধীনতা বেশি" (Information Minister Hasan Mahmud Said – Media Freedom in Bangladesh Is More Than in the United Kingdom). July 4. https://www.bbc.com/bengali/news-48864319.

Bdnews24. 2018. "Sec 57 Was a 'Tool to Curb Freedom of Speech', Law Minister Anisul Admits." January 30. https://bdnews24.com/bangladesh/sec-57-was-a-tool-to-curb-freedom-of-speech-law-minister-anisul-admits.

Bergman, David. 2015. "Bangladeshi Spies Accused of Blocking Media Adverts." *Aljazeera*, October 7. https://www.aljazeera.com/indepth/features/2015/10/bangladeshi-spies-accused-blocking-media-adverts-151005083755483.html.

Bergman, David. 2018. "Bangladesh: Ex-Chief Justice Alleges He was 'Forced' to Resign." *Aljazeera English*, September 28. https://www.aljazeera.com/news/2018/09/bangladesh-chief-justice-alleges-forced-resign-180927103453932.html.

Brown, Trevor L., and Charles R. Wise. 2004. "Constitutional Courts and Legislative-Executive Relations: The Case of Ukraine." *Political Science Quarterly* 119 (1): 143–169.

Burke, Jason. 2014. "Bangladesh PM Hints at Fresh Polls If Violence Ends." *The Guardian*, January 6. https://www.theguardian.com/world/2014/jan/06/bangladesh-election-sheikh-hasina-wajed-fresh-polls-violence.

Chopra, Surabhi. 2015. "The International Crimes Tribunal in Bangladesh: Silencing Fair Comment." *Journal of Genocide Research* 17 (2): 211–220.

Dawn. 2009. "UN to Help Bangladesh Planning War Crimes Trial Planning." April 8. https://www.dawn.com/news/904714/un-to-help-bangladesh-war-crimes-trial-planning.

Dhaka Tribune. 2017. "Sinha Resigns as Chief Justice." November 11. https://www
.dhakatribune.com/bangladesh/2017/11/11/chief-justice-sk-sinha-resigns/.
Dhaka Tribune. 2022. "PM Hasina: Bangladesh Media Is Free to Criticize My
Government." September 28. https://www.dhakatribune.com/bangladesh/2022/09
/28/pm-hasina-bangladesh-media-is-free-to-criticize-my-government.
Diamond, Larry. 2022. "All Democracy Is Global: Why American Can't Shrink from
the Fight for Freedom." *Foreign Affairs*, September 6. https://www.foreignaffairs
.com/united-states/all-democracy-global-america-cant-shrink-fight-freedom-larry
-diamond.
Economist. 2011. "The Opposition BNP Threatens to Boycott the 2014 Election." July
14. https://country.eiu.com/article.aspx?articleid=578305642&Country=Bangladesh
&topic=Politics&subtopic=Recent+developments&subsubtopic=The+political
+scene:+The+opposition+BNP+threatens+to+boycott+the+2014+election.
Economist. 2019. "Obituary of a Democracy: Bangladesh." January 30. https://espresso
.economist.com/0390aff9c68eeb7b64fbebe21c878de3.
Galhotra, Sumit. 2015. "Mission Journal: Bangladeshi Press Reined in as Hasina Exerts
Authority." Committee to Protect Journalists (CPJ). March 26. https://cpj.org/2015
/03/mission-journal-bangladeshi-press-reined-in-as-pri/.
Grynbaum, Micahel, and Eileen Sullibvan. 2019. "Trump Attacks the Times, in a Week
of Unease for the American Press." February 2. https://www.nytimes.com/2019/02
/20/us/politics/new-york-times-trump.html.
Harman, Edward, and Noam Chomsky. 1988/2002. *Manufacturing Consent: The
Political Economy of the Mass Media*. New York: Pantheon.
Human Rights Watch (HRW). 2011. "Letter to the Bangladesh Prime Minister
Regarding the International Crimes (Tribunals) Act." May 18. https://www.hrw.org
/news/2011/05/18/letter-bangladesh-prime-minister-regarding-international-crimes
-tribunals-act.
Human Rights Watch (HRW). 2018. *No Place for Criticism: Bangladesh Crackdown on
Social Media Commentary*. New York: HRW. May 9. https://www.hrw.org/report
/2018/05/10/no-place-criticism/bangladesh-crackdown-social-media-commentary
Islam, Fakhrul. 2020. "In Ten Years, Salaries and Allowances of Government
Employees Tripled (in Bengali)." *Prothom Alo*, June 20.
Levitsky, Steven, and Lucan Way. 2002. "The Rise of Competitive Authoritarianism."
Journal of Democracy 13 (2): 51–65.
Levitsky, Steven, and Lucan Way. 2010. *Competitive Authoritarianism: Hybrid
Regimes After the Cold War*. New York: Cambridge University Press.
Levitsky, Steven, and Daniel Ziblatt. 2018. *How Democracies Die*. New York:
Broadway.
New Age. 2023. "'Editors' Council Worried." March 31. https://www.newagebd.net/
article/198173/editors-council-worried.
Parvez, Saimum. 2022. "Understanding the Shahbag and Hefajat Movements in
Bangladesh: A Critical Discourse Analysis." *Journal of Asian and African Studies*
57 (4): 841–855.
Rabee, Safquat. 2019. "A Deeper Look at the Bangladesh Election." *Aljazeera English*,
January 2. https://www.aljazeera.com/opinions/2019/1/2/a-deeper-look-at-the
-bangladesh-election.
Rashid, Muktadir. 2018. "Khaleda Jailed for Five Years." *New Age*, February 9. https://
www.newagebd.net/article/34366/article/articlelist/323/index.php.

Riaz, Ali. 2013. "The Curse of the Two-Thirds." *Dhaka Tribune*, December 22. https://archive.dhakatribune.com/uncategorized/2013/12/22/the-curse-of-the-two-thirds.

Riaz, Ali. 2017. "Constructing and Deconstructing Narratives: Shahbag and Islamist Politics." In *Lived Islam and Political Islam in Bangladesh*, edited by Ali Riaz. Dhaka: Prothoma. 107–138

Riaz, Ali. 2019. *Voting in Hybrid Regime: Explaining the 2018 Bangladeshi Election*. Singapore: Palgrave Macmillan.

Riaz, Ali. 2021. "Politician-Bureaucrat Conflict from a Different Point of View." *Prothom Alo English*, July 6.

Riaz, Ali. 2023. *What's Happening: Trends and Patterns of the Digital Security Act 2018 in Bangladesh*. Dhaka: Centre for Governance Studies. January. https://freedominfo.net/content-details/4268.

Riaz, Ali, and Mohammad Sajjadur Rahman. 2021. *Who Owns the Media in Bangladesh*. Dhaka: Centre for Governance Studies. January. https://bdmediaowners.com/wp-content/uploads/2021/01/Full-Report_Who-Owns-the-Media-in-Bangladesh.pdf.

Riaz, Ali, and Fahmida Zaman. 2022. "Living Under the 'Sword of Damocles': Experiences of Journalists under a Hybrid Regime." In *Masks of Authoritarianism: Hegemony, Power and Public Life in Bangladesh*, edited by Aril Engelsen Rudd and Mubashar Hasan. Singapore: Palgrave Macmillan. 37–56

Roessler, Philp G., and Marc M. Howard. 2009. "Post-Cold War Political Regimes: When Do Elections Matter." In *Democratization by Elections*, edited by Staffan I Lindberg. Baltimore, MD: Johns Hopkins Press. 101–127

RSF. 2023. "Bangladesh." https://rsf.org/en/country/bangladesh.

SACW. 2010. "Bangladesh High Court Show Cause on Government re Constitutionality of ICT Act Powers to Block Websites." http://www.sacw.net/article1543.html.

Sarkar, Ashutosh. 2011. "Caretaker System Declared Illegal." *The Daily Star*, May 11. https://www.thedailystar.net/news-detail-185142.

Sattar, Maher. 2016. "Bangladesh Editor Faces 79 Court Cases After an Unusual Confession." *The New York Times*, March 27. https://www.nytimes.com/2016/03/28/world/asia/bangladesh-editor-faces-79-court-cases-after-saying-he-regrets-articles.html.

Schedler, Andreas. 2006. "The Logic of Electoral Authoritarianism." In *Electoral Authoritarianism*, edited by Andreas Schedler. Boulder, CO: Lynne Rienner Publisher. 1–23

The Asian Age. 2018. "Khaleda Zia's Jail Term in Corruption Case Doubled to 10 Years." October 30.

The Business Standard. 2020. "Three Dozen Cases Khaleda Zia Faces." February 8. https://tbsnews.net/bangladesh/corruption/three-dozen-cases-khaleda-zia-faces-42953.

The Business Standard. 2022. "Media in Bangladesh Enjoys Total Freedom: Info Minister." June 28, 2022. https://www.tbsnews.net/bangladesh/media-bangladesh-enjoys-total-freedom-info-minister-448994.

The Business Standard. 2023a. "Editors Guild Bangladesh Condemns Prothom Alo News Undermining Independence." March 31. https://www.tbsnews.net/bangladesh/editors-guild-bangladesh-condemns-prothom-alo-news-undermining-independence-608734.

The Business Standard. 2023b. "Editors Guild Expresses Concern Over Prothom Alo Reporter Being Picked Up." March 29. https://www.tbsnews.net/bangladesh/editors-guild-expresses-concern-over-prothom-alo-reporter-being-picked-607486.

The Daily Observer. 2023. "Over 7,000 Cases Filed Under DSA: Law Minister." June 5. https://www.observerbd.com/details.php?id=422632.

The Daily Star. 2016. "PM Blasts Star Editor." February 22. https://www.thedailystar.net/country/pm-blasts-star-editor-576148.

The Daily Star. 2018a. "34 Cases Against Khaleda." February 8. https://www.thedailystar.net/backpage/34-cases-against-khaleda-zia-bnp-chairperson-bangladesh-1531510.

The Daily Star. 2018b. "Lower Courts' Freedom Undermined by 3 Rules." January 2. https://www.thedailystar.net/frontpage/lower-courts-freedom-undermined-3-rules-1513600.

The Daily Star. 2023a. "Prothom Alo Is the Enemy of AL, Democracy, Country's People: PM." April 10. https://www.thedailystar.net/news/bangladesh/news/prothom-alo-the-enemy-al-democracy-countrys-people-pm-3293596.

The Daily Star. 2023b. "191 News Sites to be Blocked for Spreading Anti-State Propaganda." January 31. https://www.thedailystar.net/news/bangladesh/news/the-unholy-agreement-3355821.

The New York Times. 2019. *Bangladesh's Farcical Vote.* January 14. https://www.nytimes.com/2019/01/14/opinion/editorials/bangladesh-election-sheikh-hasina.html.

UN News. 2012. "UN Official Calls for Bangladesh's Next Elections to be 'Peaceful, Inclusive and Credible'." December 10. https://news.un.org/en/story/2012/12/427892-un-official-calls-bangladeshs-next-elections-be-peaceful-inclusive-and-credible.

USAID. 2022. "Final Report: Assessment of the Media Sectorin Bangladesh." Contract No./Order No. GS-10F-154BA/72038819M00001; USAID Bangladesh Monitoring, Evaluation, and Learning (BMEL) Activity: Bethesda, MA:ME&A, Inc.

Zaman, Fahmida. 2018. "Agencies of Social Movements: Experiences of Bangladesh's Shahbag Movement and Hefazat-e-Islam." *Journal of Asian and African Studies* 53 (3): 339–349.

4 Bangladesh's quiet slide to autocracy

Roles of ideology and external actors

Ideology as a tool

Although the "debilitation or elimination of the political institutions" is central to autocratization, emergent autocrats need to justify their steps. Justification often acts in unison with other tools of the autocratization process, especially coercion and cooptation, but has a distinct role in providing legitimacy to the regime's emergence and survival. This is done through an ideology. Ideology, in this instance, is understood as "a set of ideas and formulations in which the legitimating messages are situated" (Dukalskis 2017, 3). The ideational measures create an environment that allows for and legitimizes the undemocratic actions of the incumbent. In the words of Dukalskis,

> authoritarian regimes craft and disseminate reasons, stories, and explanations for why they are entitled to rule. To shield justifications from criticism, authoritarian regimes also censor information they find threatening. While committed opponents of the regime may be violently repressed, ... authoritarian state keeps the majority of its people quiescent by manipulating the way they talk and think politics.
>
> (Dukalskis 2017, 1)

Understanding the role of ideology, especially in the context of autocratic rule, requires exploration of two of its distinct dimensions. The first dimension is in the frame of the dichotomy of "liberal" and "illiberal" ideas in the context of globalization and democratization. The second dimension is the construction of a narrative that not only legitimizes the would-be autocrat and later helps continue the autocracy but also weakens the opposition.

The "third wave of democracy," which took place at a spectacular pace in the 1990s, did not only offer the ideas of a set of institutions to be built and employed but also advanced some norms and values that are intrinsic to democracy. These ideas and norms included "pluralism of actors, [and] the deconstruction of [traditional] authority" (Lewis 2022, 358). It is worth noting that the marked difference between the third wave and previous waves is that it took shape within the current phase of globalization, which has not

DOI: 10.4324/9781032712048-5

only an economic aspect but a normative aspect too. The normative aspect of globalization included "spaceless internationalism and fluid and contingent identities" (Lewis 2022, 358). A combination of these normative elements constitutes the core foundation of liberal ideology. As a significant number of citizens in various parts of the world felt unsettled by these liberal ideas, especially as they have been viewed as an importation from outside and were accompanied by globalization's economic dimensions (such as marginalization of poorer segments of society), political actors and potential autocrats seized the opportunity and offered an alternative to these ideas. Their ideas packaged as an alternative ideology include "reasserting notions of authority, reifying boundaries of the political community, and a fixity of identity, defined by essentialized (sic) understanding of gender, sex, race, religion, and nation" (Lewis 2022, 538). These ideas have been packaged as a form of nationalist ideology by the Awami League, wherein the authority figure is the sovereign and savior of the nation and national identity is fixated on a particular interpretation of history. The party and its leaders provide lip service to pluralism, while the preeminence of a leader, both in the past and in contemporary times, is the key to its understanding of how history is shaped.

Lewis (2022) has perceptively shown how the autocratic leaders of South Asia have framed politics in Carl Schmitt's anti-liberal notion of friend/enemy dichotomy (Schmitt 2007). There are two elements to this construction. Firstly, constructing/identifying/portraying a group/community/political party as the "enemy," who is considered the "existential threat," not only to the incumbent leader and the party but primarily to the nation/state. Then the leader and the party evoke "war rhetoric." Once a war analogy is evoked, there is nothing short of annihilation. In the case of Bangladesh, the Awami League and its leaders have repeatedly questioned the bona fides of its archrival Bangladesh Nationalist Party and insisted that the party is opposed to the independence of the country. Although established by a freedom fighter, the party has been labeled "anti-liberation."

Prime Minister Sheikh Hasina's repeated reference to a "conspiracy" against her government, whether in 2009 (VOA 2009), 2016 (Prothom Alo English 2016), or 2023 (bdnews24 2023), which in turn transposed to a "conspiracy against the nation" (Kaler Kantho English 2023) has made herself, her party, and the nation synonymous. The second element of this dichotomous formulation is the construction of a community, often the nation. The nation is constructed either based on a particular interpretation of history, ethnicity, or religion. As such, the community is projected as homogenous and defined based on how the "other" is excluded. In Bangladesh, this ideological aspect is reflected in the reference to the Bengali nation, excluding other ethnicities and indigenous people on the one hand while erasing the differences due to class and social stratification.

The second dimension of ideology is how a narrative is created that justifies the incumbent's claim to power, even at the expense of democratic process and accountability. The ideational effort of the ruling Awami League to undermine democracy became palpable in 2009–10 when the supporters of the government insisted that development should precede democracy. This is the essence of what is described as "authoritarian developmentalism" (Arsel, Adaman and Saad-Filho 2021). The standard-bearer of this ideology promises, among other things, "national resurgence through (re)industrialization, infrastructure construction, and insulation of local communities from global economic forces" (Arsel, Adaman and Saad-Filho 2021, 261).

The Awami League (AL), since coming to power in 2009, has underscored infrastructural development as a key to their economic agenda. It embarked on several large-scale infrastructure projects, often described as "mega projects" (Rahman 2022), which have been touted as markers of development and have the potential to change the livelihoods of the people of Bangladesh. These include the Padma Bridge and the Rooppur Nuclear Power Plant; the costs of both of these projects have skyrocketed over the period. Regime supporters argued that development requires stability and continuity, which can only be achieved by the continuation of the same party in power. By 2014, the central argument of the regime was that it was delivering unprecedented economic growth, measured by the GDP growth rate. However, the data belies this claim that the growth is "unprecedented" and a success of the current regime. In fact, Bangladesh's GDP began to grow in the 1990s when the country embarked on democratization, and the success lies in the efforts of a combination of the private sector, NGOs, and the state sector. Data shows that, save for one exception (2002), the GDP growth rate was above 4% and was in an upward trend despite changes in power and bad governance. In 2006, the last year of the BNP regime, it delivered a growth rate of 6.67%, a rate that was not achieved until 2016, eight years after the AL came into power (Figure 4.1).

A false dichotomy between democracy and development was created to justify the heavy-handed, often extrajudicial, measures of the government. The debate itself served as a source of legitimacy for the government and helped sway the support of some people. But this narrative fails to mention that the growth has been highly skewed and has increased income disparity. The Gini coefficient over the last 15 years testifies to the increasing inequality. According to Bangladesh Bureau of Statistics (BBS) data, in 2010, the Gini coefficient was 0.458; in 2016, it rose to 0.483; and the latest data from 2022 shows it as 0.499. A country is considered highly unequal if the coefficient rises to 0.500. In the past decade and a half, it has moved toward being more unequal. The income share of poorer segments has declined remarkably. More than half of the total national income is now held by the 20% wealthiest people (Table 4.1).

Besides, the development projects were being funded through ever-increasing debt. In the past decade, the government has borrowed a large sum of money from both external and internal sources without considering that repayment and debt servicing will hit hard at some point in the near future and put the economy in a difficult spot. A quick look at the amount of foreign debt in the government

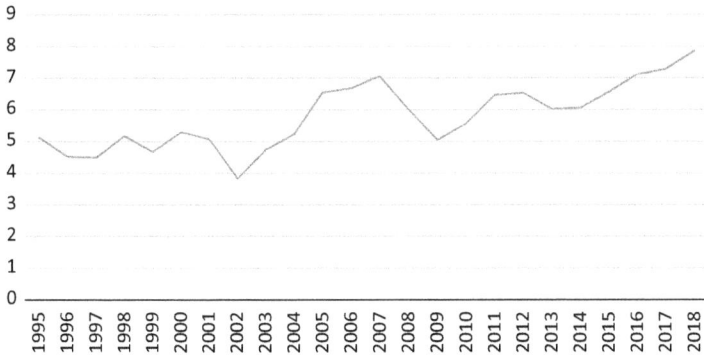

Figure 4.1 Bangladesh's GDP Growth Rate, 1996–2021.

Source: World Bank, 'GDP Growth (annual %)—Bangladesh' https://data.worldbank.org/indicator/NY.GDP.MKTP.KD.ZG?locations=BD

Table 4.1 Income Distribution, 2010–2022

Decile	2010	2016	2022
Richest 10%	35.85	38.09	40.92
Next 10%	15.94	14.86	14.62
Next 10%	11.50	11.25	10.49
Next 10%	9.06	9.06	8.36
Next 10%	7.32	7.48	6.92
Next 10%	6.01	6.24	5.81
Next 10%	5.00	5.13	4.82
Next 10%	4.10	4.05	3.88
Next 10%	3.22	2.83	2.86
Poorest 10%	2.00	1.02	1.31

Source: Bangladesh Bureau of Statistics, Household Income and Expenditure Surveys, 2010, 2016, and 2022

and private sector since June 2015 shows exponential growth. In June 2015, Bangladesh had an outstanding debt of $29.70 billion, which was accumulated over the previous 44 years; the amount rose to $69.90 billion by 2022 (Table 4.2). At least $20 billion was added in seven years. According to the World Bank, Bangladesh's foreign debt has more than tripled in the past 10 years (Ali 2022).

While the data pertaining to the economy evidently had all the signs of a brewing crisis, the ruling party and its supporters painted a rosy picture of development to justify its continuity in power even when their mandate was suspect at best. In the summer of 2022, Bangladesh experienced a serious economic downslide and was faced with shrinking foreign exchange reserves, a growing

Table 4.2 Outstanding Debt, June 2015–June 2022 (in US$ billion)

	15 Jun	16 Jun	17 Jun	18 Jun	19 Jun	20 Jun	21 Jun	22 Jun
External debt of the state sector	29.70	32.26	35.26	42.04	48.42	54.5	62.88	69.9
External debt of the private sector	7.81	8.79	10.53	13.96	14.2	14.08	18.68	25.95
Total debt	37.51	41.05	45.79	56.00	62.62	68.58	81.56	95.85

Source: Hasan 2023, 87

trade deficit, record inflation, daily depreciation of the local currency, and an intense energy crisis (Frayer 2022). The government blamed the COVID-19 pandemic and the Ukraine war for the "sudden" economic woe. But increasingly, it became evident that while the pandemic and Russian invasion might have accelerated the pace of the crisis, the regime's economic policies engendered it (Riaz 2022).

Like many other countries where democratic backsliding has taken place in the past decade, the incumbent in Bangladesh has used "patriotism" as a weapon to create schisms and as a legitimizing tool since it came into power in 2009. As mentioned before, a key issue of legitimation is creating a binary of "Us versus Them." Since 2013, the country has witnessed efforts to accentuate this division, using the term *muktijudhher chetona* (the spirit of liberation war) as a marker of that division. The concept, which literally means to uphold the ideals that underlined the 1971 war, has been used by the supporters of the ruling Awami League as an indicator of patriotism and unqualified support for the incumbent government. The 2013 Shahbag movement was coopted by the ruling party (Zaman 2018) and used to further the pernicious division. While the Shahbag movement initially emerged spontaneously, the ruling party soon coopted and made the "*muktijudhher chetona*" the battle cry. There is neither an agreed meaning to the term *muktijudhher chetona* and what it entails nor is there a way to devise a common meaning to such a nebulous idea, yet it is used as a marker of identity and as an instrument to marginalize parties, groups, and individuals for their political positions. Criticism of the notion was portrayed as unpatriotic and almost treasonous. The Shahbag movement gradually wound down, but it created the environment for a non-inclusive election, leading to the emergence of an electoral autocracy.

International support for autocratization

A large body of literature through the 1980s investigated the role of the international community in democracy promotion. This strand of studies proliferated further after the 1990s, in the context of the fall of the Soviet Union and democratization in Eastern Europe. The wave theory of democracy has highlighted the emulative impacts and the role of the international community in making democracy a global phenomenon. However, there is a conspicuous absence of the role of a global political situation and external forces in the democratic regression literature. The available literature on democratic backsliding and autocratization has almost exclusively focused on domestic factors. Explanations of democratic regression/backsliding/autocratization, as discussed in Chapter 1, have highlighted domestic political, economic, and social milieus as well as structural aspects.

Gleditsch and Ward (2006), Boix (2011), and Guntisky (2014 and 2017) have shed light on the international dimensions of the democratization process. Their work, as well as Huntington's (1991), underscored the point that democratization is not exclusively a domestic process and that international actors, systems, and organizations have roles to play. In some ways, these are more nuanced explorations of the democracy promotion thesis and the democracy promotion activities of Western countries. Gleditsch and Ward (2006), in their exploration of diffusion model, concluded that

the prospects for democracy are not exclusively related to domestic attributes but are also affected by external conditions and events. Democratization cannot be seen exclusively as a result of functionally similar processes unfolding independently within each country. Rather, international events and processes appear to exert a strong influence on democratization, consistent with our argument that external influences can change the relative power of actors and groups as well as the evaluations or relative payoffs for particular institutional arrangements.

(Gleditsch and Ward 2006, 903)

Boix's exploration focused on the relationship between democracy and development (particularly income) and reexamined the long-standing modernization thesis, which posits that "higher levels of development (measured mainly by per capita income) increase the likelihood of democratic transitions, the stability of democracies, or both" (Boix 2011). However, he showed that the "exogenous" factor plays a significant role insofar as whether a smaller country (i.e., not a great power) would be a democracy or not. In his formulation, the exogenous factor is the structure of the international order, whether it has a democratic hegemon or authoritarian hegemon will determine the rise and resilience of democratic/authoritarian hegemon. In a multipolar international order, various factors determine the role of the hegemons (Boix 2011, 814–816). As such, Boix recognizes the role of external factors, but his work does not explain why democratic regression takes place in a particular country. Guntisky (2014 and 2017) examines the relationship between wave theories—both democratic and fascist/communist—and domestic transformation from a systemic perspective and argues that volatility in the international system, manifested through abrupt hegemonic transitions, has been a major catalyst for domestic institutional reforms. Specifically, periods of sudden rise and decline of great powers, or "hegemonic shocks," create powerful incentives and opportunities for sweeping waves of domestic transformations. The fortunes of democracy, communism, and fascism in the twentieth century have been shaped by the outcomes of these geopolitical cataclysms.

(Guntisky 2014, 562)

As for the "hegemonic shocks," Guntisky suggests that there are three mechanisms through which hegemonic power brings about changes in domestic politics: coercion, influence, and emulation (Guntisky 2014, 563). By coercion, Guntisky means the imposition of a regime by the new hegemon through wars, occupations, and nation-building; influence means the expansion of networks of trade, foreign aid, patronage, and reshaping of the international institutions by the hegemon which provides benefit to the country at the receiving end; and emulation means "the process whereby a state deliberately and voluntarily imitates particular domestic institutions of successful and powerful states" (Guntisky 2014, 576). While Guntisky's principal focus is the external shock, he is not dismissive of the domestic elements that shape the system of governance, democratic or otherwise; instead, he insists that these mechanisms change the class cleavages, domestic coalitions, and institutions that lead to democratic (or conversely fascist/communist) change.

Guntisky (2014, 201) and Boix (2011), like Gleditsch and Ward (2006), have investigated the larger picture of the role of international systems in helping or impeding democracy as a global phenomenon, but how international actor(s) contribute to the backsliding remains undiscussed. Diamond (2019) takes a different path to underscore the importance of international factors in influencing the fate of democracy. Instead of explaining how the international forces shaped a democracy's global proliferation, he elucidated the current challenges faced by democracies, including in the United States. He argues that the rise of China and Russia, particularly their relentless efforts to challenge the liberal world order, has become a threat to democracy and that "the defense and advancement of democratic ideals relies on US global leadership." In this context, he also discussed how the domestic political developments in the United States have implications for global democracy. Diamond's book is more a call to action than identifying the pathway of the democratic backsliding process.

These studies provide us with clues to extrapolate as to how the international politics is a factor in the democratic backsliding, but specifically addressing the issue is still desired. Samuels (2023) has drawn our attention to this lacuna and examined the impact of the reconfiguration of global politics after the Cold War and 9/11 on politics among the main prodemocratic actors. Samuels argues that international political change since the end of the Cold War has filtered through the domestic politics of the US, the EU, and the Vatican to undermine incentives to support democracy, at least relative to the heyday of the third wave. During that earlier era, major players' support for democracy was partly a by-product of geopolitics itself, a tactical and instrumental tool in the service of the goal of fighting communism. That is, the Cold War generated incentives to promote democracy in each of the world's major prodemocratic powers. A transformed international context in recent decades has reshaped these politics, undermining such incentives.

Meyerrose (2021) insisted that it is necessary to explore the connections between the international environment and democratic backsliding, especially how the international environment precipitates domestic-level shifts. However, her work is more focused on the role of international organizations (IOs). She has insisted that IOs may have unintentionally contributed to the democratic backsliding via three mechanisms: "These organizations neglect important democratic institutions other than executives and elections when they engage in democracy promotion; they increase relative executive power at the domestic level; and they limit states" domestic policy options via requirements for membership (Meyerrose 2021, 899).

Samuel's argument that the shift in the policies of the "pro-democratic actors" as a factor in democratic backsliding is extremely important, but it is also worth noting that there has been a major shift in liberal democratic norms and narratives across the globe. Norms of liberal democracy such as liberty, freedom, and civil rights have been challenged by counter-norms, e.g., state security, civilizational diversity, and traditional values, reshaping the international environment (Cooley 2015, 50). It is easily discernible that counter narratives have been taking hold that "democracies are corrupt and worn out" and "the future, therefore, lies with stronger, more efficient authoritarian regimes, e.g., China" (Diamond 2022, 5). These narratives are not abstract ideas but have practical implications as they have facilitated the rise of both civilian and military autocrats. Additionally, the normative changes are supported by alternative providers of international public goods. The rise of China with a deep pocket and funding for infrastructure development is a case in point. Economic aspects of the rise of populist leaders and autocrats in many parts of the world have been underscored by analysts. The argument, in large measure, has been that economic globalization has limited domestic policy options and thus constrained democratically elected leaders in serving their citizens, which has been viewed by a large population as a downside of democracy. It is also argued that neoliberal economic policies have engendered deep disparity within societies, which in turn has become the source of the rise of populist leaders undermining democratic norms.

While there is an emerging consensus among academics and analysts that international factors play roles in democratic backsliding, Carothers and Press (2022) disagree with such a proposition, especially the influence of the rise of Russia and China as an overarching factor. They write,

> Unquestionably, Russia's and China's growing power and assertiveness are hurting democracy's global fortunes. They are aggressively working to undermine shared understandings of norms and using or threatening force to undermine democratically elected governments, as in Russia's invasion of Ukraine.
> Yet as a sweeping explanation of global democratic backsliding, the Russia and China factors fall short. In many of the major cases of backsliding, Russian and/or Chinese influence on national political life is simply not a major factor.
>
> (Carothers and Press 2022, 7)

The international context of autocratization, however framed, is important to understanding the global picture, but it is also important to examine the particular situation of countries where democracy has experienced serious decline. Bangladesh's autocratization process has been influenced by the overall global political situation, but I argue that it has accentuated, perhaps succeeded, because of its neighbor India's unqualified support for the incumbent since 2009. China, despite its contestation with India in extending its sphere of influence in the region, has also notably sided with the Hasina regime. Additionally, the Western nations' unwillingness to make democracy a priority for several reasons has allowed the situation to spiral downward.

How India became the catalyst

Bangladesh's relationship with India, which played a pivotal role in the birth of the country in 1971, has gone through ups and downs prior to 2009. It is generally observed that the relationship between these countries becomes closer when the AL is in power in Bangladesh and the Indian National Congress (INC) in India. Notwithstanding the personal relationship between the leaders of these parties, they also share ideological affinities. On the other hand, the Indian establishment has always viewed the Bangladesh Nationalist Party (BNP) as "unfriendly" to India. BNP's position within domestic politics has also been described as "anti-Indian," as the party used anti-Indian nationalist rhetoric to rally its supporters. In 2009, as Hasina came to power for the second term (the first term being 1996–2001), the relationship with India began to warm up. There is a clear indication that India was pivotal in the power transition from the 2007–8 military-backed government to the AL. In his memoir, then Indian External Affairs Minister Pranab Mukherjee (who later became the President) informs that he had provided assurance to then military chief General Moin U Ahmed in 2008 that he (Mukharjee) would ensure General Moin's safety after Hasina's return to power (Mukharjee 2017, 114–115). Within a year, India's security concern that Bangladesh provides a safe haven for the Northeast Indian insurgents was addressed by the Bangladesh government. Support for these insurgents ceased, and many leaders were arrested and handed over to India (Rahman 2016, 382). Various Western countries, particularly the United States, were supportive of the warm relationship, as India was the linchpin of US South Asia policy. Post-9/11 security cooperation with India was enhanced, as was economic cooperation.

However, the relationship between Bangladesh and India was increasingly becoming lopsided as legitimate demands of the former were ignored by the latter, although Dhaka was meeting New Delhi's demands. Two key issues, the sharing of water from common rivers and India's border security forces' disproportionate use of lethal force on the border, were discussed with no substantive progress. The trade deficit continued to rise in favor of India. The relationship was officially repeatedly described as "a golden era" (Dhaka Tribune 2017; Law 2018), but observers continued to question whether Bangladesh had conceded more than what it received from India (Kabir 2015).

While domestic developments within Bangladesh were indicative of democratic backsliding, particularly after 2011, India (often referred to as the "largest democracy of the world") was hardly concerned, and the US paid little attention. In 2013, with the election approaching, the opposition parties took a firm position that they would boycott the election unless the caretaker government system was restored. The US administration, EU, United Nations, and other international actors were concerned that such a non-inclusive election would be detrimental to the democratic process. Yet, India did not budge. It rebuffed the US's move, particularly by the US Ambassador to Dhaka Dan Mozena. The External Affairs Minister of India, Salman Khurshid, suggested the US should be viewing the Bangladesh situation through India's prism. He said, "India's understanding of Bangladesh will help the US" and "while the US is at some distance from Bangladesh, India is right next to it" (Dikshit 2013). It is against this background that Indian Foreign Secretary Sujatha Singh made a 21-hour trip to Dhaka on 4 December 2014. She was quite unequivocal that "India will neither broker a deal nor mediate between the opposition BNP and the ruling AL" (The Telegraph Online 2013). Meanwhile, she arm-twisted the Jatiya Party led by H M Ershad, to join the election. Singh met General H M Ershad, the leader of the Jatiya Party (JP), and reportedly "convinced" him to join the poll. Up until the meeting, the JP was having an internal squabble about whether to join the elections, and Ershad had already declared that his party would stay out of the polls. He continued to hold his position, but soon after the meeting, he was taken to the hospital by the elite police force Rapid Action Battalion (RAB). JP was the only opposition party to join the poll. An election boycotted by the remainder of the opposition took place, in which more than half of the parliament members were elected without opposition and without casting a single vote. India was quick to congratulate Sheikh Hasina and her party on their victory. The unequivocal support amounted to a direct intervention and took place despite warnings that democracy was being eroded under the Hasina regime.

Following four years, the Bangladesh-India relationship became closer despite the change of guard in New Delhi from the INC to the Bharatiya Janata Party (BJP). As the Narendra Modi regime began to dismantle the edifice of Indian democracy and push the country toward autocracy, there was no reason to hope that it would have a critical approach to the precipitous decline of democracy in Bangladesh. Bangladeshi opposition parties, especially the BNP, accepted the decisive role of India and visited India ahead of the election to build trust (Haider 2018). These efforts proved to be in vain. Well, before the 2018 electoral process began, there were signs that the Awami League government would not risk a free election. Despite the fact that the opposition succeeded in cobbling together an alliance under octogenarian jurist Kamal Hossain, persecution of the opposition continued, freedom of expression continued to dwindle, and all symptoms of an autocracy became evident. Bureaucratic obstructions to the deployment of international observers were insurmountable, forcing the Asian Network for Free Elections (ANFREL) to abandon its plan to send observers. The European Union (EU) also refrained from sending its team.

In 2018, although it was evident to the Indian establishment that the Awami League had already "assiduously subverted democratic norms and institutions" and that in a fair election "the Awami League will be reduced to an embarrassing minority in the next Parliament" (Chakravarti 2018), India's support for the Awami League remained unflinching. On the other hand, Bangladesh's ruling AL has become so dependent on India that Foreign Minister AK Abdul Momen has said that he has made requests to India to ensure the survival of the Hasina regime at any cost (The Business Standard 2022).

Why India supports the Hasina regime

India's unequivocal support for the Hasina regime, despite obvious democratic erosion over the years, was guided by four considerations. First, India's regional hegemonic ambition with an eye to being a global player. India has always considered South Asia its backyard and intended to have unrestrained control over its smaller neighbors. Its role in 1971 in Bangladesh was partly driven by its humanitarian and partly strategic considerations, but its annexation of Sikkim (1975), intervention in Sri Lanka's civil war (1987–90), repeated blockade of Nepal (1989 and 2015), and military action during coup in the Maldives (1988) are indicative of its hegemonic desire.

India has considered its neighborhood as perilous and intended to have control over the developments. This has led to a negative view of India in the region (Ganguly 2020), where neighbors believe that India pursues its own interests at the expense of democracy in the respective countries.

Secondly, India has several security concerns that influence its actions. For decades, India had faced insurgencies in the Northeastern states, which became difficult to stem due to a lack of direct, easy land access to the region necessary for security operations. Ostensibly, the insurgents received support from Bangladesh during the BNP's reign. The geographical reality that only land connects India's eight northeastern states with its mainland is through a 12–14-mile corridor located between China and Bangladesh known as the Siliguri Corridor (also known as Chicken's Neck) has weighed heavily on India's behavior. The small corridor can become a choke point if China and Bangladesh work together. India's added security concerns has been the presence of some local and regional militant groups in Bangladesh. Thirdly, there are economic and material benefits, which I will delve into shortly. Fourthly, the geopolitics of rivalry with China. India is afraid of China's potential influence on Bangladesh, particularly in the last decade with the rise of an assertive China. Finally, Narendra Modi's penchant for populist authoritarianism. Given that India itself is witnessing shrinking freedom of expression, a decline in human rights, and institutional decay, Modi and the BJP would prefer to have a neighbor that emulates it rather than shine with democratic credentials. That will make India's state of governance pale by comparison.

As for material and financial benefits, the list is long, but a few are worth noting. During the past 14 years, India has secured transit through Bangladesh (Byron and Palma 2019), gained permanent access to two main ports in the Bay of Bengal (Saxena 2023), signed an energy deal which ensures that Bangladesh buys electricity at the highest price (Mahmud 2023), inked an agreement which allows India to install a surveillance system in the Bay of Bengal (Chowdhury 2019), reached a water-sharing deal which provides India control over the river Kushiyara (Prothom Alo English 2022), and Feni engaged in close defense cooperation (Chaudhury 2022), while trade gaps increased in favor of India (The Financial Express 2022). There has been very little reciprocation from India, as even Hasina acknowledged in 2018, saying that India will remember forever what Bangladesh gave it (Prothom Alo English 2018).

China as the facilitator

It is not surprising that China has emerged as a supporter of the Hasina regime, considering that it fits China's vision of a new global order and aligns with the ideology of authoritarianism. What is intriguing is that it did so despite rivalry and contestation with India, which is the current Bangladesh government's primary backer. This has made China a facilitator of the autocratic transformation.

The relationship between Bangladesh and China has been a low-key matter for decades, despite China being the largest supplier of weapons to Bangladesh since 1978. Cooperation has gradually expanded over the past decades, and trade has increased, although with a significant trade deficit in China's favor. The close relationship accelerated since Sino-Indian maritime rivalry intensified. China has viewed Bangladesh as a littoral state of the Indian Ocean Region and Bay of Bengal Region and understands its strategic importance. "China considers ports on the Bay of Bengal to have strategic value" (Anwar 2021). It became one of the major investors in Bangladesh's infrastructural development projects after 2009. In 2014, Bangladesh agreed to a Chinese proposal to build a deep seaport at Sonadia (bdnews24 2014), but later moved away due to India's concerns. Before the 2014 election, China called for a "smooth election." In a carefully worded statement, a Foreign Ministry spokesperson "called on the relevant parties to settle disputes through dialogue, ensure a smooth election, and work together for political and social stability and economic development" (Global Times 2013). But China turned around soon afterward to seize the opportunity of building a better relationship with Bangladesh in the backdrop of Western states' criticisms of the election. Despite the disappointment regarding the deep seaport, China began aggressively courting Bangladesh thereafter. Resultantly, in 2016, Bangladesh joined the Belt and Road Initiative (BRI), bought two submarines, and signed 26 memoranda of understanding valued at $24.45 billion during the visit of Chinese President Xi Jinping. It described the relationship as a "strategic partnership" (Karim and Liton 2016).

China has become a major source of funding for various infrastructural development projects in Bangladesh under the present government. This funding, like in many other countries in the world, has become an instrument of influence. Analyzing the nature and impacts of these kinds of investments around the globe, the Center for International Private Enterprise (CIPE) has coined the term "corrosive capital" (CIPE 2018), which means "financing, whether state or private, that lacks transparency, accountability, and market orientation." Most importantly, this capital "[originates] from authoritarian regimes" and "exploits and exaggerates governance gaps to influence economic, political, and social developments in recipient countries" (CIPE n.d.). Goldstein and Hontz noted,

> Historically, Corrosive Capital flows stem from authoritarian regimes and are inextricably linked to adverse governance outcomes in recipient countries. Corrosive Capital infiltrates vulnerable democracies, inciting debt dependencies, achieving underlying political motives, and yielding negative impacts on local communities and private sectors. These flows enter recipient countries through exploitable legal structures and are safeguarded and enabled by corruption and cronyism.
>
> (Goldstein and Hontz 2021, 2)

Such a role of China's investments has been noticed in various countries, including Sri Lanka in South Asia (Attanayake 2023), Slovakia and the Czech Republic (Šimalčík 2021) in Central Europe and in North Macedonia, Serbia, Bosnia and Herzegovina, and Montenegro in the Balkans (Marusic 2021). It is well documented that China's investments and loans to various countries are opaque, which leads to corruption. In Bangladesh, it has allowed the Hasina government to reward its supporters by doling out money on projects that are plagued by a lack of oversight, the absence of public consultations, or a competitive and transparent procurement and bidding process. In addition to enriching supporters, the proceeds of corruption also help to fund the ruling party's machinery at the local and national level, providing it with an electoral advantage.

China has not been shy to demonstrate its growing power, as reflected in the request by the Chinese Defense Minister in April 2021 that Bangladesh should not join any military alliance outside the region (The Economic Times 2021) and warned against joining the Quadrilateral Security Dialogue (Quad) or risk "substantial damage" to the relationship (Radio Free Asia 2021). Although Bangladesh officially rebuffed it, the government of China has not retracted its comments, and the relationship has become closer.

These developments made India so uncomfortable that in 2018, Prime Minister Hasina had to reassure India that it need not worry about Bangladesh-China ties (The Times of India 2018). But by then, the US seemed to have taken note of the growing influence of China in Bangladesh. In 2019, the US's Indo-Pacific Document noted Bangladesh as an "emerging partner" (US Department of Defense 2019).

The failure of the UN and the negligent West

Since the end of 2012, the European Union, its member states, the United Nations, and other international bodies have begun to express concerns and have requested that the Bangladesh government engage in dialogue with the opposition to hold an inclusive and fair election. Oscar Fernandez Taranco, a senior official of the Political Office, was dispatched by the UN Secretary General in late 2012 to mediate between political parties. He made three trips until December 2013. But his missions failed, and no action from the UN followed. Several high-profile officials from the US, UK, and other countries visited Dhaka and met the government and opposition. For example, the UK's Senior Foreign Office Minister, Baroness Warsi, made a trip in December, which was preceded by Nisha Bishal Desai, the US Assistant Secretary of State for South and Central Asian Affairs, in November. Despite these trips and repeated calls, Hasina remained unfazed and went ahead with the unilateral election. She, however, promised to hold another election soon "if the opposition stops violent protests" (Burke 2014).

After the 2014 election, the spokesperson for the UN Secretary General issued a statement expressing sadness "by the loss of life and incidents of violence" but making no reference to any future steps (UN 2014). Reactions from the US and Western countries were largely muted, although a few countries condemned the violence during the election. The reaction of the United Kingdom (Foreign and Commonwealth Office 2014) is a case in point. The entire election process, which was no less than a sham, was not outright rejected.

The reaction of the US was a little different, especially considering its approach to Bangladesh. Bangladesh had not featured prominently in US foreign policy in the previous decade. It appears that "stability" and a "moderate" regime in the third-largest Muslim majority country were the primary considerations. These came to the forefront because, during the BNP's rule between 2001 and 2006, several Islamist militant groups emerged, some with regional connections. Besides, in the post-9/11 period, the US was focused on Afghanistan and Iraq after the 2003 invasion. India became a proxy for the US. However, as mentioned before, by the summer of 2013, it became increasingly clear that there was a disagreement between the US and Indian positions on the upcoming election issue in Bangladesh. US efforts to shift India's position failed. The US clearly took note of the absence of the opposition in the election. On June 6, Marie Harf, the Deputy Department Spokesperson of the State Department, issued a press release that said,

> The United States is disappointed by the recent Parliamentary elections in Bangladesh. With more than half of the seats uncontested and most of the remainder offering only token opposition, the results of the just-concluded elections do not appear to credibly express the will of the Bangladeshi people.
>
> While it remains to be seen what form the new government will take, United States commitment to supporting the people of Bangladesh remains undiminished. To that end, we encourage the Government of Bangladesh and opposition parties to engage in immediate dialogue to find a way to hold as soon as possible elections that are free, fair, peaceful, and credible, reflecting the will of the Bangladeshi people.
>
> (US Department of State 2014)

Interestingly, the entire election process, which was no less than a sham, was not outright rejected. There was an overwhelming impression that the 2014 election would be an exception, and soon the ruling party would change its course.

The slide toward autocracy not only continued but also accelerated. In the following years, as Donald Trump came into power in the US and the overall global state of democracy declined, Europe was reeling under the

Brexit imbroglio, extreme rightwing groups began to gain salience in France and Germany. Hasina continued to enjoy explicit and tacit support with little criticism while legal and extralegal measures were implemented to establish complete control over all the state institutions.

Ahead of the 2018 election, the international community repeatedly called upon the government for an inclusive, credible, acceptable, and fair election, almost akin to the situation in 2013–14. But the country witnessed a repeat of the 2014 election, albeit with new tactics. The participation of the opposition made no difference because the electoral management was already set in favor of the incumbent. The rigging of the election was quite blatant, which raised hope among the many Bangladeshi political activists and observers of Bangladeshi politics that the international community would demonstrate a more robust response.

The predictable congratulatory messages came from India, China, Russia, and the Middle Eastern monarchies. From Western governments, there were initial muted and muffled criticisms. The United States Department of State expressed concerns about "credible reports of harassment, intimidation, and violence;" the United Kingdom urged "a full, credible, and transparent resolution of all complaints related to the conduct of the elections;" and the EU noted the "significant obstacles to a level playing field [...] throughout the [election] process [which] have tainted the electoral campaign and the vote" (Paul and Siddiqui 2019). US President Donald Trump's letter 17 days after the election lacked a congratulatory note and highlighted the "international calls for independent investigations into the 30 December, 2018, national election" (The Daily Star 2019).

But the overall message from Western governments indicated their willingness to "work with the new government" without mounting any pressure on Sheikh Hasina to reverse course. In the subsequent years, many commentators were still baffled and searched for an explanation for the passivity on the part of these governments. The answer to this question may be found in an overarching foreign policy strategy. In hindsight, it is evident that these countries adopted a strategy referred to as "engagement."

Notwithstanding that the term is often criticized as a "vexing, mutable, all-purpose word," and there is a longstanding debate on its merits, the essential argument is that it is better to work with recalcitrant states to obtain leverage that might influence their behavior rather than to isolate them and adopt punitive policies. As international relations experts put it, "engagement [is a] foreign policy strategy which depends to a significant degree on positive incentives to achieve its objectives" (Haass and Sullivan 2023, 113). It is argued that "the distinguishing feature of the American engagement strategies is their reliance on the extension or provision of incentives to shape the behavior of the countries with which the US has important disagreements."

The increasing use of the engagement strategy in the post-Cold War era can be attributed to the rise of various regional actors and the diminishing influence of the US in global politics. In the case of Bangladesh, this was largely influenced by the increasing geostrategic importance of the country along with the growing influence of China in the region.

While these considerations and the strategy of engagement guide the Western approach to the new Bangladesh government, particular situations further constrain their capacity to maneuver. These include the ongoing anti-terrorism efforts of the Bangladeshi government.

Although the Bangladesh government publicly denied the existence of transnational terrorist groups in the country, both Al Qaeda and the Islamic State (ISIS) made marks within the country. The Holey Artisan Cafe attack on 1 July 2016, was a worrying development for the international community as it posed a threat to global security. The need for enhanced security cooperation with the Government of Bangladesh became significant, and the success of the Hasina government in taming the militants therefore played in its favor.

The presence of Rohingya refugees in Bangladesh was another factor that helped the Awami League government sway international support. As Bangladesh had been shouldering the refugee burden since August 2017 without any negative impacts on the interests of Western countries, the governments favored the status quo. The Rohingya crisis became an important justification for Western governments to skirt their responsibilities in seeking to support democracy. The business interests of various Western countries also triumphed over their concerns for democracy. The US, which has a very large trade deficit with Bangladesh, began pursuing an offer to sell weapons to Bangladesh, and trade between the two countries has increased in the past year. The EU, which is the largest market for Bangladeshi ready-made garment (RMG) exports, did not want to destabilize the cheap source of products purchased by their consumers. In addition, Bangladesh's economic growth in the past decades offers the country an opportunity to become a new destination for private investments as an emerging market. All of these require stability, or, in other words, the status quo. This essentially served the autocratization process.

The preceding discussion on the four elements of autocratization showed how these factors sometimes acted in tandem and took the country down a path away from democracy. By 2023, as the country is gearing up for another election, the incumbent is hell-bent on maintaining the status quo and ensuring another victory.

References

Ali, Mohammad. 2022. "Bangladesh's Foreign Debt More Than Triples in 10 Years." *The Business Standard*, December 7. https://www.tbsnews.net/economy/bangladeshs-foreign-debt-more-triples-10-years-547358.

Anwar, Anu. 2021. "As US, China Fight Over Bangladesh, India Is the Real Winner." *The Diplomat*, January 21. https://thediplomat.com/2023/01/as-us-china-fight-over-bangladesh-india-is-the-real-winner/.

Arsel, Murat, Fikret Adaman, and Alfredo Saad-Filho. 2021. "Authoritarian Developmentalism: The Latest Stage of Neoliberalism?" *Geoforum* 124: 261–266.

Attanayake, Chulanee. 2021. *Sri Lanka's Economic Crisis: Lessons for Those in China's Debt*. New Delhi: Observer Research Foundation. March 2. https://www.orfonline.org/expert-speak/sri-lankas-economic-crisis/.

Attanayake, Chulanee. 2023. "Sri Lanka's Lessons for Economies in Debt Distress" *ORF Issue Brief 627*. New Delhi: Observer Research Foundation.

bdnews24. 2014. "Sonadia Deep Sea Port Board." June 8. https://bdnews24.com/economy/sonadia-deep-sea-port-on-board.

bdnews24. 2023. "Hasina Alerts Citizens to 'Conspiracy to Usurp Power' Before Election." January 6. https://bdnews24.com/politics/80osu7r297.

Boix, Carles. 2011. "Democracy, Development, and the International System." *American Political Science Review* 105 (4): 809–828.

Boix, Carlos, Michael Miller, and Sebastian Rosato. 2013. "A Complete Data Set of Political Regimes, 1800–2007." *Comparative Political Studies* 46 (12): 1523–1554.

Burke, Jason. 2014. 'Bangladesh PM Hints at Fresh Polls if Violence Ends." *The Guardian*, January 6. https://www.theguardian.com/world/2014/jan/06/bangladesh-election-sheikh-hasina-wajed-fresh-polls-violence.

Byron, Rejaul Karim, and Primol Palma. 2019 "India's Transit Thru' Bangladesh: Reaping Benefit Is a Challenge." *The Daily Star*, November 29. https://www.thedailystar.net/frontpage/india-bangladesh-trasit-route-challenge-reap-benefit-1833220.

Carothers, Thomas, and Benjamin Press. 2022. *Understanding and Responding to Global Democratic Backsliding*. Washington, DC: Carnegie Endowment for International Peace.

Chakravarty, Pinak Ranjan. 2018. "Shadow of India, Hasina Government's Corruption, Repression of BNP Looms over Bangladesh Polls." Commentary, 9 September. New Delhi: Overseas Research. https://www.orfonline.org/research/43844-shadow-of-india-hasina-governments-corruption-repression-of-bnp-looms-over-bangladesh-polls/

Chaudhury, Dipanjan Roy. 2022. "India, B'desh Sign First Defence Deal Under $500m LC." *The Economic Times*, September 7. https://economictimes.indiatimes.com/news/defence/india-bdesh-sign-first-defence-deal-under-500m-lc/articleshow/94059712.cms?utm_source=contentofinterest&utm_medium=text&utm_campaign=cppst.

Chowdhury, Kamran Reza. 2019. "Bangladesh Gives India Greenlight to Install Surveillance Radar System." *Eurasia Review*, October 8. https://www.eurasiareview.com/08102019-bangladesh-gives-india-greenlight-to-install-surveillance-radar-system/.

CIPE. 2018. "Channeling the Tide: Protecting Democracies Amid a Flood of Corrosive Capital." Washington D.C.: CIPE. https://www.cipe.org/wp-content/uploads/2018/09/MXW_CIPE_CorrosiveCapitalPaper_PRIN_20190809.pdf

CIPE. n.d. *Corrosive & Constructive Capital Initiative*. Washington, DC: CIPE.

Cooley, Alexander. 2015. "Authoritarianism Goes Global: Countering Democratic Norms." *Journal of Democracy* 26 (3): 49–63.

Dhaka Tribune. 2017. "Sinha Resigns as Chief Justice." November 11. https://www.dhakatribune.com/bangladesh/2017/11/11/chief-justice-sk-sinha-resigns/.

Diamond, Larry. 2019. *Ill Winds: Saving Democracy from Russian Rage, Chinese Ambition and American Complacency*. New York: Penguin.

Diamond, Larry. 2022. "All Democracy Is Global." *Foreign Affairs* Centennial Issue (October): 182–197.

Dikshit, Sandeep. 2013. "India's understanding of Bangladesh will help U.S." *The Hindu*, December 30. https://www.thehindu.com/news/national/indias -understanding-of-bangladesh-will-help-us/article5516435.ece.

Dukalskis, Alexander. 2017. *The Authoritarian Public Sphere: Legitimation and Autocratic Power in North Korea, Burma, and China*. London: Routledge.

Foreign and Commonwealth Office, UK. 2014. "Baroness Warsi Comments on Bangladesh Election Results." January 6. https://www.gov.uk/government/news/ baroness-warsi-comments-on-bangladesh-election-results.

Frayer, Lauren. 2022. "How Bangladesh Went from an Economic Miracle to Needing IMF Help." *NPR*, November 9. https://www.npr.org/2022/11/09/1134543648/ bangladesh-economy-imf-loan.

Ganguly, Sumit. 2022. "India Is Paying the Price for Neglecting its Neighbors." *Foreign Policy*, June 23. https://foreignpolicy.com/2020/06/23/india-china-south -asia-relations/.

Gleditsch, Kristian Skrede, and Michael D. Ward. 2006. "Diffusion and the International Context of Democratization." *International Organization* 60 (4): 911–933.

Global Times. 2013. "China Calls for Smooth Election in Bangladesh." November 27. https://www.globaltimes.cn/content/828114.shtml.

Goldstein, Adam, and Eric Hontz. 2021. *Corrosive Capital: Known Unknowns*. Washington, DC: CIPE.

Guntisky, Seva. 2014. "From Shocks to Waves: Hegemonic Transitions and Democratization in the Twentieth Century." *International Organization* 68 (3): 561–597.

Gunitsky, Seva. 2017. *Aftershocks: Great Powers and Domestic Reforms in the Twentieth Century*. Princeton, NJ: Princeton University Press.

Haass, Richard N., and Meghan L. O'Sullivan. 2000. "Terms of Engagement: Alternatives to Punitive Policies." *Survival* 42 (2): 113–135. https://www.brookings .edu/wp-content/uploads/2016/07/2000survival.pdf.

Haass, Richard N., and Meghan L. O'Sullivan. 2023. "Terms of Engagement: Alternatives to Punitive Policies." *Survival* 42 (24): 113–135.

Haider, Suhasini. 2018. "BNP Seeks India's Help for Free and Fair Polls in Bangladesh." *The Hindu*, June 8. https://www.thehindu.com/news/international/ bnp-seeks-indias-help-for-free-and-fair-polls-in-bangladesh/article24107694.ece.

Huntington, Samuel. 1991. *The Third Wave: Democratization in the Late 20th Century*, Norman, OK: University of Oklahoma Press.

Kabir, Humayun. 2015. "Changing Relations between Bangladesh and India: Perception in Bangladesh." In *India and South Asia: Regional Perspectives*, edited by Vishal Chandra. New Delhi: Pentagon Press. 29–45.

Kaler Kantho English. 2023. "Bangladesh Faces National and International Conspiracy." April 13. https://www.kalerkantho.com/english/online/national/2023/04/13/51826.

Karim, Rezaul, and Shakhawat Liton. 2016. "Strategic Partners." *The Daily Star*, October 15. https://www.thedailystar.net/frontpage/strategic-partners-1298923.

Law, Abhishek. 2018. "PM: It's the Golden Era of India-Bangladesh Relations." *Businessline*, May 25. https://www.thehindubusinessline.com/news/indo-bangladesh -relations-going-through-a-phase-of-golden-era-modi/article23993395.ece.

Lewis, David G. 2022. "Autocratization as an Ideological Project: Carl Schmitt's Anti-Liberalism in South Asia." In *Routledge Handbook of Autocratization in South Asia*, edited by Sten Widmalm. London: Routledge. 357–367.

Mahmud, Faisal. 2023. "Bangladesh in Hot Seat Over Adani's Power Deal." Aljazeera. March 30. https://www.aljazeera.com/economy/2023/3/30/bangladesh-in-a-hot-seat-over-adanis-power-deal#:~:text=Bangladeshi%20media%20reported%2C%20citing%20BPDB,in%20Payra%2C%20Banskhali%20or%20Rampal.

Marusic, Damir. 2021. *Corrosive Capital in the Western Balkans: An Analysis of Four High Impact Chinese Investments*. Washington, DC: CIPE. May. https://www.cipe.org/resources/corrosive-capital-in-the-western-balkans-an-analysis-of-four-high-impact-chinese-investments/.

Meyerrose, Anna M. 2021. "International Sources of Democratic Backsliding." In *Routledge Handbook of Illiberalism*, edited by Andras Sajo, Renata Utiz, and Stephen Holmes. New York: Routledge.888–906.

Mukharjee, Pranab. 2017. *The Coalition Years 1996–2012*. New Delhi: Rupa Publications.

Prothom Alo English. 2016. "Hasina Still Sees Conspiracy by Anti-Liberation Forces." March 17. https://en.prothomalo.com/bangladesh/Hasina-still-sees-conspiracy-by-anti-liberation.

Prothom Alo English. 2018. "India will remember forever forwhat Bangladesh gave it: PM Hasina." May 31. https://en.prothomalo.com/bangladesh/India-will-remember-forever-for-what-Bangladesh.

Prothom Alo English. 2022. "Bangladesh, India Reach Consensus on Kushiyara Water Sharing." August 25. https://en.prothomalo.com/bangladesh/e4rwt0pdsn.

Radio Free Asia. 2021. "China Warns of 'Damage' to Relations if Bangladesh Joins Quad Initiatives." May 10. https://www.rfa.org/english/news/china/bangladesh-quad-05102021174758.html.

Rahman, Mohammad Sajjadur. 2016. "Bangladesh and its Neighbors." In *Routledge Handbook of Contemporary Bangladesh*, edited by Ali Riaz and Mohammad Sajjadur Rahman. London: Routledge. 378–388.

Rahman, Shaikh Abdur. 2022. "Mega Development Projects in Bangladesh: Key Objectives and Stakeholders." *India Briefing*, April 25. https://www.india-briefing.com/news/mega-development-projects-in-bangladesh-to-create-competitive-market-for-investors-24830.html/.

Riaz, Ali. 2022. "Bangladesh's Economic Crisis: How Did We Get Here?." South Asia Source, Atlantic Council. August 5. https://www.atlanticcouncil.org/blogs/southasiasource/bangladeshs-economic-crisis-how-did-we-get-here/.

Ruma, Paul, and Siddiqui, Zeba. 2019. "EU, US Denounce Bangladesh Election Violence, Irregularities." *Reuters*, January 1. https://www.reuters.com/article/bangladesh-election/eu-us-denounce-bangladesh-election-violence-irregularities-idUSL3N1Z10D0.

Samuels, David J. 2023. "The International Context of Democratic Backsliding: Rethinking the Role of Third Wave 'Prodemocracy' Global Actors." *Perspectives in Politics* 21 (3): 1001–1012.

Saxena, Ankit. 2023. "Explainer: Unlocking India's North East to Bay of Bengal Through New Transit Agreement with Bangladesh." *Swarajya*, May 14. https://swarajyamag.com/infrastructure/explainer-unlocking-indias-north-east-to-bay-of-bengal-through-new-transit-agreement-with-bangladesh.

Schmitt, Carl. 2007. *Concept of the Political*. Chicago, IL: Chicago University Press.

Šimalčík, Matej. 2021. *Oligarchs and Party Folks Chinese Corrosive Capital in Slovakia and Czechia*. Bratislava, Slovakia: Central European Institute of Asian Studies. https://ceias.eu/wp-content/uploads/2021/07/Oligarchs-and-Party-Folks.pdf.

The Business Standard. 2022. "Media in Bangladesh Enjoys Total Freedom: Info Minister." June 28. https://www.tbsnews.net/bangladesh/media-bangladesh-enjoys-total-freedom-info-minister-448994.

The Daily Star. 2019. "Trump Wishes Hasina Success in Third Term." January 26. https://www.thedailystar.net/frontpage/news/trump-greets-hasina-re-election-1693111.

The Economic Times. 2021. "China, Bangladesh Should Oppose Powers from Outside the Region Forming 'Military Alliance' in South Asia: Chinese Defence Minister." April 29. https://economictimes.indiatimes.com/news/defence/china-bangladesh-should-oppose-powers-from-outside-the-region-forming-military-alliance-in-south-asia-chinese-defence-minister/articleshow/82289339.cms?utm_source=contentofinterest&utm_medium=text&utm_campaign=cppst.

The Financial Express. 2022. "Reducing Bangladesh's Trade Gap with India." October 20. https://thefinancialexpress.com.bd/editorial/reducing-bangladeshs-trade-gap-with-india-1666279118.

The Telegraph Online. "India Not to 'Broker' Dhaka Deal - Sujatha: Would Like to See Maximum Participation." December 5. https://www.telegraphindia.com/world/india-not-to-broker-dhaka-deal-sujatha-would-like-to-see-maximum-participation/cid/238173.

The Times of India. 2018. "India has Nothing to Worry about China-Bangladesh Ties: Sheikh Hasina." February 21. http://timesofindia.indiatimes.com/articleshow/63011441.cms?utm_source=contentofinterest&utm_medium=text&utm_campaign=cppst.

United Nations. 2014. "Statement Attributable to the Spokesperson for the Secretary-General on Bangladesh." January 6. https://www.un.org/sg/en/content/sg/statement/2014-01-06/statement-attributable-spokesperson-secretary-general-bangladesh.

US Department of Defense. 2019. *Indo-Pacific Strategy: Preparedness, Partnership and Promoting a Networked Region*. Washington, DC: Department of Defense. June 1. https://media.defense.gov/2019/jul/01/2002152311/-1/-1/1/department-of-defense-indo-pacific-strategy-report-2019.pdf.

US Department of State. 2014. "Parliamentary Elections in Bangladesh: Press Statement." January 6. https://2009-2017.state.gov/r/pa/prs/ps/2014/01/219331.htm.

VOA. 2009. "Sheikh Hasina Talks about Conspiracy to Foil the Elected Government." March 28. https://www.voabangla.com/amp/a-16-2009-03-28-voa18-94448039/1398053.html.

Zaman, Fahmida. 2018. "Agencies of Social Movements: Experiences of Bangladesh's Shahbag Movement and Hefazat-e-Islam." *Journal of Asian and African Studies* 53 (3): 339–349.

Conclusions
Is the Bangladesh case unique? What's next?

In the past decade, four interrelated elements, separately but concurrently, contributed to Bangladesh's autocratization process. The country's propitious second beginning of democratization in 2009 reversed course within a short period. Having witnessed earlier rounds of civilian and military authoritarian rule, Bangladesh's current brush with authoritarianism is not new, but even by its own standard, the nature and scope of the post-2011 slide have been extraordinary. Institutional changes, the media's complicity, investing an ideology to legitimize the rule, and external actors' intrusive role have incrementally weakened state institutions, stifled freedom of expression, limited the space for dissention, decimated the civil society, and withered the rule of law. Constitutional and extra-constitutional measures have been used for executive aggrandizement, particularly to concentrate power in the hands of Prime Minister Sheikh Hasina. Hasina's supporters and associates have acknowledged such concentration of power as a sign of strength, with her son and IT advisor Sajeeb Wazed saying in 2018 that "authoritarian is a badge of honor" to her (Paul, Das and Siddiqui 2018) and the Economist describing her as "Asia's iron lady" (Economist 2023a).

In the preceding chapters of this book, I have explored both endogenous and exogenous factors in this transformation. The exploration of the pathway to Bangladesh's autocratization raises two questions: is Bangladesh's democratic backsliding different from the global phenomenon, and what is in store for the future of the country? The first question, to some extent, asks whether the four elements of autocratization have relevance to explaining the experiences of other countries that are undergoing a similar phenomenon.

As a large body of existing studies on democratic backsliding have demonstrated, institutional changes, often through amending the constitution, are a key to democracy's slow death. Turkey's constitutional change in 2017, which introduced an executive Presidency, not only shifted power from the legislative to the executive branch, but essentially removed checks and balances and accountability mechanisms of the head of the government. But in fact, such aggrandizement began well before the formal changes: as early as 2012, Recep Tayyip Erdogan was exercising executive power akin to that of a president (Varol 2015). In Venezuela, the 2000 Constitutional Amendments

DOI: 10.4324/9781032712048-6

under Hugo Chavez were the beginning of the country's authoritarian journey, which continued through four terms of his presidency and until his death in 2013. As his successor Nicolas Maduro's behavior clearly demonstrates, Chavez's legacy endures, with electoral manipulation by the incumbent being laid bare with the 2020 election (Galgano 2021). In Hungary, a new constitution in 2012 reshaped the power structure and provided Viktor Orban and his party Fidsez with unchecked power (BBC 2013). In Poland, the ruling PiS party's constitutional maneuvering has enabled it to run amok. Between 2010 and 2013, the Polish regime instituted 12 constitutional amendments that generated 728 acts, which received a further 466 amendments. In Zambia, 2016 constitutional amendments enhanced presidential powers and continued a long history of broken promises on constitutional reform (Hinfelaar 2021).

The institutional changes are not limited to simply ensuring the lack of accountability but also creating a weapon to weaken state institutions, particularly the judiciary. Poland's judicial independence was curtailed through constitutional provisions, repeated purges, and court packing. In Thailand, the constitutional court has protected the military and its undemocratic behavior as the country witnessed the erosion of democracy. In the Philippines, President Rodrigo Duterte removed then-Chief Justice Maria Lourdes Sereno in 2018 after she entertained a challenge to the regime's so-called "war on drugs." Justices sympathetic to the regime were appointed during Duterte's tenure. The weakening of judicial independence is also palpable in countries where the democratic façade has been maintained. For example, in India, Narendra Modi's regime has taken steps and allegedly used unlawful tactics to create a subservient judiciary (Meyerrose 2021, 893).

Persecution of opposition using state institutions is a hallmark of autocratic regimes. In Bolivia, during three presidential terms between 2005 and 2019, Evo Morales not only presided over the severe erosion of democratic practices but also weaponized the judicial system to silence the opposition. In Turkey, after the abortive coup of 2016, the Erdogan regime arrested thousands of opponents, from political activists to academics. The European Commission reported in 2021 that

> More than 130,000 public servants, including 4,156 judges and prosecutors, as well as 29,444 members of the armed forces were summarily removed from their jobs for alleged membership in or relationships with "terrorist organizations" by emergency decree-laws subject to neither judicial nor parliamentary scrutiny.
>
> (Stockholm Center for Freedom 2022)

In India, the Modi regime's relentless efforts since 2014 to weaken the opposition by all means are easily discernible. Rahul Gandhi's removal from Parliament in 2022 due to his conviction for making defamatory remarks about Prime Minister Modi, is a testimony to how the judicial system is being used. Another example is the use of government investigation agencies against opposition leaders for alleged financial crimes.

Hungary's Viktor Orban is far from alone in creating a pliant mediascape since his ascendance to power. Parliament has passed laws that limit the media's independence, and the agency that oversees the media and broadcasting has become a political tool. Poland's largest public broadcaster has been taken under government control since the PiS came into power in 2015. Its stated objective to "repolonize" and eliminate Western influence has turned the entire mediascape into a propaganda machine. In Turkey, the incumbent has taken over the mediascape by buying independent media and using unseen influence mechanisms. A 2022 Reuters report revealed, "Directions to newsrooms often come from officials in the government's Directorate of Communications, which handles media relations, more than a dozen industry insiders told Reuters. The directorate is an Erdogan creation, employing some 1,500 people and headquartered in a tower block in Ankara" (Spicer 2022). Additionally, the Turkish mediascape has been influenced by other tools, including the purchase of previously independent media. A Reuters investigation showed that

> "the biggest media brands are controlled by companies and people close to Erdogan and his AK Party (AKP) following a series of acquisitions starting in 2008. State advertising revenue is funnelled (*sic*) largely to pro-government publications, a Reuters examination of the data found. Conversely, government-appointed regulators direct penalties for breaching Turkey's media code almost exclusively to independent or opposition news providers, a Reuters review of these penalties showed. Criticizing the president and alleging official corruption can fall foul of regulators."
>
> (Spicer 2022)

As India slides toward electoral autocracy, its media are either being attacked, bought, or simply cowed down. In 2023, a raid by tax officials on the BBC office and the purchase of the critical television channel NDTV by Gautam Adani, a businessman known to be close to Modi, are just two recent examples. In the Philippines, under Duterte, television stations were forced off the air and newspapers were sued. While emerging autocrats used coercion and legal measures to silence critics and put restrictions on mass media and social media, in almost all instances, they also found journalists and media willing to play to the tune of the regime. In many cases, the media's support was because of its ideological affinity with the rulers.

Ideology, either constructed or reconfigured to suit the needs of the emerging autocrats, is the key to gaining support both from the media and general society. "[Autocratic] governments work hard to develop and maintain a 'hegemonic discourse'—circulating ideas, tropes, and narratives in society to promote the ruling elite's values and norms and to legitimise (*sic*) their hold to power" (Lewis 2022, 364). Hindutva in India, constructed by Bharatiya Janata Party (BJP) and pursued vigorously by Narendra Modi regime; a brand of Islamism propagated by the AKP and Erdogan in Turkey, Chavismo of Hugo Chavez in Venezuela, and Viktor Orban's particular form of ethnona-tionalism in Hungary—all have been used to justify personalistic autocratic rule and mobilize people in support of the regime's anti-democratic measures. Anti-pluralist ideologies have shaped the political discourse, created schisms within society, and modeled a binary of patriot and enemy of the state. These and other similar ideologies have not only justified the regime's rule but also presented the leader as the savior of the nation. Majoritarianism has replaced the essence of democracy by treating all citizens equally. Populism of differ-ent hues has portrayed liberal democratic values as inimical to the interests of the people and thus justified transgressions as a service to the people and for the "greater good."

Institutional changes, media acquiescence, and ideological hegemony—three elements of the autocratization process that have been in play in various countries—can also be seen in the case of Bangladesh in the past decade. As such, Bangladesh's autocratization pathway is not unique but rather consistent with the autocrat's playbook. However, the Bangladesh case stands out from others insofar as the role of external actors. As I have demonstrated in the pre-ceding chapter, India's interjection and China's facilitatory role accelerated the autocratization process while Western countries remained silent. Indeed, an international environment supporting autocrats, the ideological battle between autocracy and democracy, the complacency of the democratic forces (especially of the United States), and the weakening of Western hegemony have continued to play a part in the democratic backsliding, but the direct involvement of a country in propping up an autocratic rule in another country is extraordinary. The closest to such an interjection that we see is the role played by Russia to its neighbor Belarus during the 2021–2022 anti-Alexander Lukashenko popular uprising. The Belarus-Russia relationship since the dis-solution of the Soviet Union has been complex, as reflected in the Belarusian efforts in the 1990s to maintain a neutral stance between NATO and Russia. Belarusian leader Lukashenko condemned the Russian annexation of Crimea in 2014 and alleged ahead of the 2020 election that Russia was trying to stir chaos in Belarus. There were also other instances of divergence and tension between these two countries, but when Lukashenko faced massive protests after the 2020 election (considered by the international community as highly rigged), he turned to Russia for help. Putin provided diplomatic help and said that he stood by Lukashenko. Additionally, he offered Russian "reserve" forces to quell the demonstrations (Livesay 2020). Russian help also came in the form of journalists, technicians, and anchors after Belarusian journalists went on strike in state-owned television stations during the pro-democracy protests in 2020–2021 (Balmforth and Zheguleb 2020). With the protection of the Lukashenko regime in 2020, Russia has secured Belarus' subservience, and it is increasingly becoming a "vasal state" of Russia (Hopkins 2023). Perhaps a direct intervention to protect an autocrat is destined to shape the relationship between two countries.

What is in store for Bangladesh?

While it is important to understand how Bangladesh's journey toward autocracy proceeded, it is equally vital to consider where the country is headed. Considering the pathways of autocratic regimes around the world, there are two alternative scenarios for the country. The first alternative is to continue the status quo, while the second is to change course.

The status quo scenario, however, does not mean that the country will remain in the same political condition for an indefinite period. Most countries that witnessed the erosion of democratic qualities and democratic backsliding tend to progress further toward autocratization. Often, hybrid regimes, that is, those that maintain the veneer of democracy while all other autocratic traits dominate the governance, manage to remain in this state for a few years, but they gradually descend to an autocratic regime. Freedom House's "The Nations in Transit" report of 2022 showed that in Central Europe and Central Asia, eight countries that entered the grey zone of hybrid regimes have not left the category between 2004 and 2022 (Freedom House 2022), while a few have descended into autocracy.

In this regard, two Asian examples are given: Cambodia and Myanmar. Cambodia's democratic journey began with a UN-supervised and mediated election in 1993. Since then, the country has incrementally moved toward a de facto one-party state under Hun San. The main opposition party was banned by judicial action in 2017 ahead of the 2018 election, while severe repression has succeeded in silencing critics. Although elections are held at regular intervals, they only serve to provide legal and constitutional legitimacy to the incumbent. The 2018 election delivered a one-party parliament (Morgenbesser 2019). After the opposition emerged from the ashes of the banned Cambodia National Rescue Party (CNRP) and formed the Candlelight Party (CP) in 2019, it too faced severe obstacles. In February 2023, the last independent media in Cambodia was shut down, and in March, opposition leader Kem Sokha was sentenced to 27 years of house arrest. In May, the National Election Committee barred Candlelight Party from contesting in the July 2023 polls. The election, although participated in by 17 other parties, was just a one-party show.

With the election in 2015, Myanmar appeared to have embarked on a democratization process and became a hybrid regime under the leadership of Aung San Suu Kyi, where the military held the tutelary power. But in February 2021, the military staged a coup, and the country returned to a closed autocracy as a popular uprising against the regime was brutally quelled. These examples show that hybrid regimes often descend into autocracy. Like

Cambodia, the forthcoming election in Myanmar is "expected to be neither free nor fair, given the current political environments" (International IDEA 2023a, 17).

As such, for Bangladesh, the status quo scenario implies further debilitation of institutions, continued concentration of power in the hands of Sheikh Hasina in the short term, and the transformation of the country into a de facto one-party state. However, the durability of such a system remains doubtful, and the modus operandi of succession in and transition from such a system remains uncertain. Apparent stability, better described as enforced stability, has an ingrained seed of volatility.

The second option for the country is to reverse the course of autocratization. Although the claims that "democracies are turning the tide" (The White House 2023) and that "autocrats are now on the back foot" (Power 2023) are too optimistic, there are a few countries that have successfully transitioned into democracy or are *en route* in the past years. Despite powerful autocratic leaders maintaining their grip over power in their respective countries and their attempts to export their model, there is a way out of autocracy. According to one account, between 2000 and 2021, nine countries transitioned into democracy from an authoritarian spell (Otaloa 2022). Varieties of Democracy Institute's 2023 report informs that "out of top 10 democratizing countries in the last 10 years, eight were autocracies in 2012. By 2020, the situation is reversed; eight out of these ten are democracies in 2022" (V-Dem 2023, 27).

Bangladesh's incumbent regime, like many others around the world, is unlikely to voluntarily correct course and hold a free and fair election, as this may result in its losing power. There is little incentive for the incumbent to create a path for democratization. The V-Dem report identified five elements as key to the successful reversal of the autocratization trend: "large-scale popular mobilization against incumbent; judiciary reversing executive takeover; unified opposition coalescing with civil society; critical elections and key events bringing alteration in power; and international democracy support and protection" (V-Dem 2023, 31). While not all of these have taken place in each instance, at least one of these elements has been active. Drawing on this lesson, one can ask whether Bangladesh's situation suggests that any of these will happen in the coming months.

Severe repression, muzzling of media, court packing, and the successful propagation of a development narrative have muted any popular mobilization against the regime for years. However, the economic crisis since the middle of 2022 has created a sense of desperation among a large section of the citizens. Opposition political parties paralyzed by the government's machinations have begun to take to the streets. Since May 2023, political parties have gained traction, and rallies of the opposition parties, especially the BNP, have become larger. While these developments indicate growing displeasure against the incumbent, as of August 2023, a critical mass is missing for a ground swell against the government. In previous popular uprisings, both before and after independence, the urban middle class served as the driving force of popular movement, while the lower middle class and working populace joined the mobilization. Such a situation is yet to emerge. But popular uprisings around the world, both successful and unsuccessful, seldom follow a predictable pattern; they tend to be spontaneous and precipitous. Bangladesh's history also bears this out. One key uncertain element of a possible mass upsurge is the continuance of the economic crisis, especially the unabated price hike of essential commodities. A significant portion of Bangladeshi citizens believe that the country's economy is heading in the wrong direction. A survey titled "The State of Bangladesh's Political Governance, Development and Society," jointly conducted by The Asia Foundation, Bangladesh, and the BRAC Institute of Governance and Development (BIGD), published on 29 August 2023, revealed that as much as 70% of the respondents think Bangladesh's economy is heading in the wrong direction (BIGD 2023). In another survey, conducted by the International Republican Institute (IRI), 51% described the economic situation as very bad and bad (IRI). The government's claim that the economic situation is under control belies the facts. With debt skyrocketing and double-digit inflation pushing the citizens to the brink (Taiyeb 2023), the country may reach the tipping point in the near future, especially in the wake of the election. As Rudd (2023) noted, "The most dreaded situation from the rulers' perspective is one in which a severe economic downturn mobilizes large numbers of ordinary people into protest or at least into refusing to accept the prospect of another term for Sheikh Hasina and her team" (Rudd 2023).

The likelihood of the judiciary acting to reverse executive aggrandizement is almost nonexistent in Bangladesh for several reasons, including its lack of independence. Although on paper the judiciary (especially the higher judiciary) is independent from the executive, its role has been far from such. Before retiring, one Chief Justice said, "Constitutionally, the judiciary is independent. But in reality, we all know and understand how much" (The Daily Star Bangla 2023). The sentiment is echoed in a report of the Law Commission submitted to a Parliamentary Standing Committee. The report says the independence of the judiciary has remained a pie in the sky (Karim 2023). The Annual Report on Human Rights by the US Department noted "serious problems with the independence of the judiciary" and "corruption and political interference compromised its independence (US Department of State 2022). It is alleged that in the past decade, court packing has been unprecedented, even by Bangladesh's standards. Recent events highlight the state of the judiciary. On 6 August 2023, 18 lawyers went to a bench of the High Court to file a petition for anticipatory bails after cases were filed against them in the wake of pandemonium and vandalism in the Supreme Court Bar Association office. Two previous benches declined to entertain their petition. A two-member HC bench finally agreed to hear the petition the next day. The lawyers urged that a court issue a verbal order immediately so that they were not arrested. One judge remarked that there was no point in issuing a verbal order because previously people have been arrested despite being on bail, and those arrested were tortured in police custody. The judge remarked, "the High Court does not have that standing anymore" (News Bangladesh 24). While this statement reflects the judge's disappointment, comments from other judges demonstrate their complete political alignment with the executive branch. On 15 August 2023, in a public event to commemorate the death anniversary of Sheikh Mujibur Rahman, Supreme Court judges delivered speeches laced with political messages supporting the ruling party. Two judges of the Appellate Division described themselves as "oath-bound politician" (New Age 2023).

Since March 2023, the opposition parties have been holding identical demonstration programs demanding an election under a caretaker government. Although the "one-point" movement reflects coordination and liaison among the opposition parties, they have not succeeded in coalescing and forming a common platform. Unless the opposition can overcome their current fragmentation and reinvigorate civil society (however small), the future of any united movement to unsettle the government seems weak. With uncertainty surrounding the three factors that have contributed to the reversal of democratic backsliding in other countries, Bangladesh is left with two options: turning the tide through elections and/or through international support for the revival of democracy.

Considering the important role of elections in the turnaround, Bangladesh's upcoming polls, expected to be held in early 2024, have become an issue of serious contention. There is widespread apprehension among observers of Bangladeshi politics that the next election will be a repeat of 2014 and 2018, albeit with new kinds of machination by the ruling party. As discussed previously, the current constitutional arrangements regarding the conduct of the election are so skewed toward the incumbent that a level-playing field is nonexistent, and unless the system is changed, Sheikh Hasina's victory is a foregone conclusion. The opposition parties are demanding the restoration of the caretaker system, or something akin to it, to ensure a free, fair, and inclusive election—a call the ruling party has repeatedly rejected. The politicization of administration has created a group within the civil service and members of law enforcement agencies who would prefer the current power arrangement to continue. The cost of defeat for the supporters of the ruling party and the beneficiaries of the past decade's spoiled system has become high. Rudd (2023) has identified the beneficiaries as "the armed forces, the security agencies, the courts, the administration, much of the media, and most of the business class."

The possible future trajectories of Bangladeshi politics, particularly the upcoming election, have attracted unprecedented international attention. By mid-2023, global powers such as the United States, China, and Russia had become embroiled in a tug-of-war, while the long shadow of India, Hasina's primary backer, continued to loom large. In early 2022, the US began to express its displeasure regarding the human rights situation in Bangladesh and underscored the need to hold a free and fair election. In 2022 and 2023, several high-level State Department officials visited the country and sounded the warning bell. For example, in March 2022, US Under Secretary of State for Political Affairs Victoria Nuland underscored the issue of democracy as a key point in the relationship between these two countries (Chowdhury 2022); in January 2023, Assistant Secretary of State for South and Central Asian Affairs Donald Lu reiterated the message; and in February 2023, US State Department Counsellor Derek Chollet said that erosion of democracy in any country, including Bangladesh, limits Washington's ability to cooperate with that country (The Business Standard 2023c). Besides, Secretary of State Antony Blinken told Bangladesh's Foreign Minister A.K. Abdul Momen in April 2023 that the world was watching Bangladesh's upcoming election (The Daily Star 2023). The European Union has expressed similar sentiments.

It was against this background that the US announced a new visa policy for Bangladesh on 24 May 2023 (US Department of State 2023). The purpose of the new visa policy was to support a fair election in Bangladesh and those trying to restore the democratic system. Under this new policy, the US will be able to deny visas to those who obstruct the election process in Bangladesh. The actions to be considered "obstructions" to the electoral process and those who will come under them are clearly laid out. Vote rigging, voter intimidation, the use of violence to prevent people from exercising their right to freedoms of association and peaceful assembly, and the use of measures designed to prevent political parties, voters, civil society, or the media from disseminating their views are listed as acts of obstruction. Those who will come under the purview of the new policy include current and former Bangladeshi officials, members of pro-government and opposition political parties, and members of law enforcement, the judiciary, and security services. While the new visa policy is not a punitive measure and is fraught with problems of implementation, it has sent a clear message that, unlike 2014, the US intends to pursue its policy to see that a democratic process is restored. In the face of criticisms of repressive measures and growing calls from the US and its Western allies to ensure a credible free election, Prime Minister Hasina has ramped up her disparagement of the United States and alleged several times that the US was trying to topple her (scroll 2023; Dhaka Tribune 2023)—an allegation the US has denied.

China, on the other hand, intensified its diplomatic initiatives in support of the incumbent. In the first six months of 2023, three top Chinese foreign affairs officials visited Bangladesh. Chinese Foreign Minister Qin Gang made a surprise stopover in Dhaka in the middle of the night, just before Assistant Secretary Donald Lu's visit to Bangladesh in January (Sharma 2023). Chinese Special Envoy to Myanmar Deng Xijun arrived in Dhaka in April, just a day before Foreign Minister Momen was to visit Washington. And soon after the US announced the new visa policy, Chinese Vice Minister of Foreign Affairs Sun Weidong visited Dhaka for three days. Additionally, on 14 June 2023, Chinese Foreign Ministry Spokesperson Wang Wenbin extended support to Sheikh Hasina's remarks against the US and, without referring to any particular country, said, "we stand ready to work together with Bangladesh and other countries to oppose all forms of hegemonism and power politics" (Chinese Embassy in Bangladesh 2023).

Russia's interest in supporting the Hasina government is tied to its economic interests and its ideological stance of supporting nondemocratic regimes worldwide. Russia is currently building Bangladesh's only nuclear plant in Rooppur, which will cost $12.38 billion, of which $11.38 is provided by Russia as a loan to Bangladesh. Bangladesh, on several occasions, has abstained from UNGA votes against the Russian invasion of Ukraine, and Sheikh Hasina decried US sanctions against Russia (The Telegraph Online 2022). Russia was one of the countries that congratulated Hasina soon after the 2014 and 2018 elections. In December 2022, the Russian Embassy in Dhaka overtly criticized US Ambassador Peter Haas in a tweet involving a spat between the Bangladesh Government and the US Embassy. Ambassador Haas, on 14 December, made a visit to the home of a victim of enforced disappearance. During his visit to the victim's house, the US envoy was confronted by a group of people, ostensibly with the support of the ruling party, demanding justice for those who were executed after military trials, allegedly for engaging in coup attempts in 1977 during Ziaur Rahman's rise to power. The actions of the group irked the envoy and were considered a security threat. This led to uncomfortable exchanges between the Bangladesh government and the US State Department, including a phone call from Deputy Secretary of State Wendy Sherman. The Russian Embassy in Dhaka in a tweet suggested that the visit was an example of US meddling in Bangladesh's domestic policies. The exchanges between these two embassies on cyberspace took a turn when the Russian Foreign Ministry spokesperson alleged that the US and Western envoys in Bangladesh are "persistently trying to influence" the domestic processes (New Age 2022). In July 2023, as calls from the lawmakers of the United States and Europe for an inclusive election grew louder, a Russian Foreign Ministry spokesperson took a swipe at the US and other Western nations and described their concerns as "neocolonialism" (Eruygur and Sakib 2023).

While the US versus China-Russia war of words has heated up, as of the time of writing this book, Indian officials had maintained silence on whether they would continue to support the Hasina regime in the coming election. Visits by Indian Foreign Secretary Vinay Khatra in February 2023 and Foreign Minister Subrahmanyam Jaishankar in April and May, and Indian Prime Minister Narendra Modi's invitation to Hasina to be an observer at the G20 Summit to be held in New Delhi in September 2023, demonstrate that India has yet to put pressure on Bangladesh for a free and fair election. The question that will determine India's role is whether it intends to take a position divergent from the US. In some measures, India has been put in a precarious position. On the one hand, it has complex and multifaceted relationships with the US, which it needs to strengthen for its global aspirations, while on the other, it has a regional preference for the Hasina regime—India's most reliable regional ally. The former necessitates alignment with the US and support for the endeavor to have a democratic Bangladesh, while the latter dictates unqualified support for the continuation of the current political dispensation in Bangladesh. Also worth mentioning is China's growing influence in Bangladesh, which makes New Delhi nervous. This should serve as an incentive for India to support the US and the Western nations' efforts to restore an accountable system in Bangladesh. India's business interests, for example, as a large source of remittances and a market for Indian products, also predicate its inclination toward the current regime. Prime Minister Narendra Modi and India's ruling Bharatiya Janata Party's (BJP) penchant for authoritarianism, combined with the Indian security establishment's erroneous assumption that a democratic Bangladesh would facilitate the rise of security challenges for India, have shaped its Bangladesh policy since 2009. Although this has created an enforced stability and engendered predictability in Indo-Bangladesh government-to-government relations, anti-India sentiment among common people has flourished (Ethirajan 2021; Mostofa 2022; Banerji 2023). For Indian leadership, the question is whether to take a long view of its relationship with Bangladesh or make it conditional on one leader (Gambhir 2023).

The contestation between the global powers in Bangladesh on the issue of democracy is, in large measure, shaped by the ongoing contest between India, China, and the US in the Indo-Pacific region. Each of these countries intends to establish its control over the sea lanes in the Pacific and Indian Oceans. The Bay of Bengal and its potential to play a key role in the strategic power configuration and economic activities in the Indo-Pacific region have accelerated the contest. Despite the Hasina regime's inclination toward India for survival and support, its increasing reliance on and growing ideological affinity with China have accentuated the tension. Ostensibly, China's objective in Bangladesh is to keep the country away from the US sphere of influence, exploit a large market, and create a debt trap.

The US-China rivalry, or in other words, a clash between ideologies of inclusive and non-inclusive governance, has serious implications for democracy in Bangladesh and the future trajectory of the country. As Bangladesh approaches its election, the incumbent is likely to face further internal pressure, thanks to the increasing economic crisis, the outside actors who would like to see a course correction. The election, if held like two previous ones, will not only bolster Sheikh Hasina and the Awami League in terms of legal and constitutional power but will also provide them the opportunity to decimate the opposition, leading to a one-party state like Cambodia. Besides, unlike 2014 and 2018, an engineered election will create instability, violence may immediately follow, and international repercussions are very likely. Therefore, if the forthcoming election is a potential key to democracy, so it may also turn the country into a closed autocracy, and the country may plunge into a long-term crisis. Thus, Bangladesh stands at a crossroads; the election may well decide whether the country will cross the Rubicon.

References

Balmforth, Tom, and Ilys Zhegulev. 2020. "Belarusian Leader Credits Russian TV for Helping Him Survive Media Strike." *Reuters*, September 2. https://www.reuters.com/article/us-belarus-election-russia-journalists/belarusian-leader-credits-russian-tv-for-helping-him-survive-media-strike-idUSKBN25T1GH.

Banerji, Anuttam. 2023. "Opposition Protests in Bangladesh Threaten Bilateral Relations with India." *South Asian Voices*, February 13. https://southasianvoices.org/opposition-protests-in-bangladesh-threaten-bilateral-relations-with-india/.

Brac Institute of Governance and Development (BIGD). 2023. *The State of Bangladesh's Political Governance, Development and Society: According to Its Citizens*. Dhaka: BIGD and the Asia Foundation. https://bigd.bracu.ac.bd/wp-content/uploads/2023/08/The-State-of-Bangladeshs-Political-Governance-Development-and-Society_According-to-Its-Citizens.pdf.

Chinese Embassy in Bangladesh. 2023. "Chinese Foreign Ministry Spokesperson Wang Wenbin's Remarks on Foreign Country's Sanctions on Bangladesh." June 14. http://bd.china-embassy.gov.cn/eng/sghd/202306/t20230614_11096467.htm#:~:text=%E2%80%9CIt%20has%20the%20power%20to,What's%20China's%20comment%3F.

Chowdhury, Shahidul Islam. 2022. "US Keen to Support Efforts to Advance Democracy in Bangladesh." *New Age*, March 21. https://www.newagebd.net/article/166046/us-keen-to-support-efforts-to-advance-democracy-in-bangladesh.

Dhaka Tribune. 2023. "PM Hasina: Maybe US Does Not Want Me in Power." May 16. https://www.dhakatribune.com/bangladesh/2023/05/16/pm-hasina-maybe-us-does-not-want-me-in-power.

Economist. 2023a. "Sheikh Hasina Is Asia's Iron Lady." May 24. https://www.economist.com/asia/2023/05/24/sheikh-hasina-is-asias-iron-lady.

Eryugur, Burc, and Sm Najmus Sakib. 2023. "Russia Claims Western Calls for 'Free, Fair' Elections in Bangladesh 'Neo-Colonialism'." *Anadolu Agency*, July 6. https://www.aa.com.tr/en/asia-pacific/russia-claims-western-calls-for-free-fair-elections-in-bangladesh-neo-colonialism-/2939082.

Ethirajan, Anbarasan. 2021. "Why Narendra Modi's Visit to Bangladesh Led to 12 Deaths." *BBC News*, March 31. https://www.bbc.com/news/world-asia-56586210.

Freedom House. 2022. *Nations in Transit 2022: From Democratic Decline to Authoritarian Aggression*. Washington, DC: Freedom House. https://freedomhouse.org/report/nations-transit/2022/from-democratic-decline-to-authoritarian-aggression.

Galgano, Kate. 2021. "Venezuela's Story: Democratic Paths to Authoritarianism." *Real Clear World*, February 24. https://www.realclearworld.com/articles/2021/02/24/venezuelas_story_democratic_paths_to_authoritarianism_661643.html.

Gambhir, Mohak. 2023. "India-Bangladesh Relations – Conditional to a Sheikh Hasina Government?." *SouthAsian Voices*, 12 September. https://southasianvoices.org/india-bangladesh-relations-conditional-to-a-sheikh-hasina-government/.

Hinfelaar, Marja. 2021. "Legal Autocratisation Ahead of the 2021 Zambian Elections." *Journal of Eastern African Studies* 16 (4): 558–575.

Hopkins, Valerie. 2023. "Belarus Is Fast Becoming a 'Vassal State' of Russia." *New York Times*, June 22 2023. https://www.nytimes.com/2023/06/22/world/europe/belarus-russia-lukashenko.html.

International IDEA. 2023a. "Democracy in Asia and The Pacific Outlook 2023." Discussion paper 1/2023. https://www.idea.int/sites/default/files/publications/democracy-in-asia-and-the%20pacific-outlook-2023.pdf.

Karim, Riadul. 2023. "Independence of Judiciary Remains Elusive (in Bengali)." *Prothom Alo*. August 29. https://www.prothomalo.com/bangladesh/apdc3qaqpv.

Lewis, David G. 2022. "Autocratization as an ideological project: Carl Schmitt's Anti-Liberalism in South Asia." In *Routledge Handbook of Autocratization in South Asia.* edited by Sten, Widmalm. London: Routledge. 357–367.

Livesay, Chris. 2020. "Putin Says Russian 'Reserve' Forces Ready to Back Lukashenko in Belarus if 'the Situation Gets Out of Control'." *CBS News*, August 27. https://www.cbsnews.com/news/belarus-news-putin-says-russian-forces-set-to-back-alexander-lukashenko-europe-last-dictator-2020-08-27/.

Meyerrose, Anna M. 2021. "International Sources of Democratic Backsliding." In *Routledge Handbook of Illiberalism*, edited by Andras Sajo, Renata Utiz, and Stephen Holmes. New York: Routledge. 888–906

Morgenbesser, Lee. 2019. "Cambodia's Transition to HegemonicAuthoritarianism." *Journal of Democracy* 30 (1): 158–171.

Mostofa, Shafi Md. 2022. "Another Anti-India Wave Sweeps Bangladesh." *The Diplomat*, June 17. https://thediplomat.com/2022/06/another-anti-india-wave-sweeps-bangladesh/#:~:text=Historically%2C%20India%20and%20Bangladesh%20have,for%20India's%20support%20in%201971.

New Age. 2022. "Russia Slams US Envoy's Role in Bangladesh." December 25. https://www.newagebd.net/article/189916/dec-14-incident-an-expected-result-of-us-envoys-activities-in-bangladesh-russia.

New Age. 2023. "Editors' Council Worried." March 31. https://www.newagebd.net/article/198173/editors-council-worried.

News Bangla 24. 2023. "High Court Does Not Have that Standing Anymore." August 6. https://www.newsbangla24.com/news/229646/That-position-of-High-Court-is-no-more-High-Court.

Otaola, Miguel Angel Lara. 2022. "Worried about the state of democracy? Here are some reasons to be optimistic instead." *Monkey Cage*, Washington Post. 2 March. https://www.washingtonpost.com/politics/2022/03/02/democracy-backsliding-authoritarianism-index/.

Paul, Ruma, Krishna N. Das, and Zeba Siddiqui. 2018. "Exclusive: For Bangladesh PM, Authoritarian Tag Is 'Badge of Honor', Son Says On Poll Eve." *Reuters*, December 29. https://www.insider.com/r-exclusive-for-bangladesh-pm-authoritarian-tag-is-badge-of-honor-son-says-on-poll-eve-2018-12.

Power, Samantha. 2023. "How Democracy Can Win: The Right Way to Counter Autocracy." *Foreign Affairs*, March/April. Online version, 16 February. https://www.foreignaffairs.com/united-states/samantha-power-how-democracy-can-win-counter-autocracy.

Rudd, Arild Engelsen. 2023. "As Elections Near, 3 Scenarios for Bangladesh." *The Diplomat*, August 14. https://thediplomat.com/2023/08/as-elections-near-three-scenarios-for-bangladesh/.

Scroll. 2023. "Sheikh Hasina Accuses US of Seeking Regime Change in Bangladesh." *Scroll.in*, April 11. https://scroll.in/latest/1047161/sheikh-hasina-accuses-us-of-seeking-regime-change-in-bangladesh.

Sharma, Umang. 2023. "Why Chinese Foreign Minister, on First Diplomatic Trip to Africa, Made Midnight Stop in Bangladesh?" *First Post*, January 11. https://www.firstpost.com/world/why-chinese-foreign-minister-on-first-diplomatic-trip-to-africa-made-midnight-stop-in-bangladesh-11965442.html.

Spicer, Jonathan. 2022. "Insiders Reveal How Erdogan Tamed Turkey's Newsrooms." *Reuters*, August 31. https://www.reuters.com/investigates/special-report/turkey-erdogan-media/.

Stockholm Center for Freedom (SCF). 2022. "Backsliding in Democracy Continues in Turkey, European Commission Says." October 14. https://stockholmcf.org/backsliding-in-democracy-continues-in-turkey-european-commission-says/.

Taiyeb, Faiz Ahmad. 2023. "What Is the Future of Bangladesh's Debt-Ridden Macroeconomy?" *The Daily Star*, May 23. https://www.thedailystar.net/opinion/views/news/what-the-future-bangladeshs-debt-ridden-macroeconomy-3327626.

The Business Standard. 2023c. "Eroding Democracy Could Limit US Cooperation with Bangladesh: US Official." February 15. https://www.tbsnews.net/bangladesh/eroding-democracy-could-limit-us-cooperation-bangladesh-us-counselor-chollet-585694.

The Daily Star. 2023c. "World Is Looking to Bangladesh for Next Election, Blinken Tells Momen." April 11. https://www.thedailystar.net/news/bangladesh/diplomacy/news/world-looking-bangladesh-next-election-blinken-tells-momen-3294251.

The Daily Star Bangla. 2022. "Constitutionally, the Judiciary Is Independent: But in Reality, We All Know and Understand How Much." February 28. https://bangla.thedailystar.net/node/208037.

The Telegraph Online. 2022. "Hasina Urges US to Withdraw Sanctions Imposed on Russia." July 8. https://www.telegraphindia.com/world/sheikh-hasina-urged-the-us-to-withdraw-sanctions-imposed-on-russia/cid/1873684.

The White House. 2023. "Remarks by President Biden at the Summit for Democracy Virtual Plenary on Democracy Delivering on Global Challenges." March 29. https://www.whitehouse.gov/briefing-room/speeches-remarks/2023/03/29/remarks-by-president-biden-at-the-summit-for-democracy-virtual-plenary-on-democracy-delivering-on-global-challenges/.

US Department of State. 2022. "2022 Country Reports on Human Rights Practices: Bangladesh." Washington D.C.: US Department of State. https://www.state.gov/reports/2022-country-reports-on-human-rights-practices/bangladesh/.

US Department of State. 2023. "Announcement of Visa Policy to Promote Democratic Elections in Bangladesh." May 24. https://www.state.gov/announcement-of-visa-policy-to-promote-democratic-elections-in-bangladesh/.

Varol, Ozan. 2015. "Presidentialism in Turkey: Is it Already Here?" *Constituionnet*, November 24. https://constitutionnet.org/news/presidentialism-turkey-it-already-here.

V-Dem. 2023. *Democracy Report 2023: Defiance in the Face of Autocratization.* Gothenburg: Varieties of Democracy Institute, Department of Political Science, University of Gothenburg. https://policycommons.net/artifacts/3455279/democracy-report-2023/4255594/.

Index

For Product Safety Concerns and Information please contact our EU
representative GPSR@taylorandfrancis.com
Taylor & Francis Verlag GmbH, Kaufingerstraße 24, 80331 München, Germany